SPLIT TRAVEL GUIDE

BEYOND

A Handbook for Exploring the Best of Split, Croatia and its Surroundings

BORISLAV BLAGOJE

Borislav Blagoje

Copyrights © 2023 Borislav Blagoje

All rights Reserved

Split Travel Guide 2023 And Beyond

TABLE OF CONTENT

TABLE OF CONTENT 2

Introduction 6

CHAPTER ONE 8

Getting to Know Split 8

    History of Split 9

    Geography 11

    People and Culture 13

    Climate 15

CHAPTER TWO 16

Top Sights and Attractions 16

    Diocletian's Palace 17

    Marjan Hill 20

    Riva Promenade 23

    Cathedral of Saint Domnius 26

    The Islands of Hvar and Brač 29

    Hvar Island 30

    Brač Island 31

Mestrovic Gallery 33

CHAPTER THREE 38

Food and Drink 38

　　Traditional Dalmatian Cuisine 38

　　Dining in Split 41

　　Local Markets and Delicacies 43

　　Croatian Wine and Wineries 46

CHAPTER FOUR 50

Nightlife and Entertainment 50

　　Bars and Pubs 50

　　Clubs and Nightclubs 52

　　Cultural Events and Performances 55

　　Live Music 57

　　Outdoor Cinemas 60

　　Sports Bars 62

CHAPTER FIVE 66

Accommodation 66

　　Luxury Hotels 66

　　Mid-Range Hotels 69

Split Travel Guide 2023 And Beyond

- Budget Hotels and Hostels 71
- Private Apartments and Vacation Rentals 74
- Guesthouses and Bed & Breakfasts 76
- Accommodation Tips 79

CHAPTER SIX 84

Lesser-Known Attractions And Experiences (Hidden Gem) 84

- Veli Varoš Neighborhood 84
- Bene Beach 87
- Joze Tea House 89
- The Froggyland Museum 91
- The Jewish Cemetery 93
- Kasjuni Beach 95
- The Green Market (Pazar) 97

CHAPTER SEVEN 102

Best Day Trips from Split 102

- Hvar Island 102
- Brac Island 105
- Trogir 107
- Omis 109

    Krka National Park 111

    Dubrovnik 113

CHAPTER EIGHT 118

Practical Information 118

    Currency and Money Exchange 118

    Tips for Managing Money in Split 120

    Transportation 121

    Language 123

    Weather and Climate 125

    Safety and Emergency Services 128

    Healthcare and Pharmacies 131

    Electrical Outlets 133

CHAPTER NINE 138

Conclusion 138

Final Thoughts and Farewells 138

Split Travel Guide 2023 And Beyond

Introduction

Welcome to the Split Travel Guide 2023, your ultimate companion for discovering the fascinating city of Split, Croatia, and its picturesque surroundings. As the second-largest city in Croatia, Split is a captivating blend of ancient history, vibrant culture, stunning natural beauty, and modern charm. This comprehensive guide will unveil the best of Split, taking you on a journey through its enchanting streets, world-class attractions, and breathtaking landscapes.

Nestled on the eastern shores of the Adriatic Sea, Split is renowned for its well-preserved historical sites, such as the impressive Diocletian's Palace, which dates back to the Roman Empire. The city's rich cultural heritage, however, goes beyond its ancient origins, as it continues to thrive with lively markets, modern art galleries, and a bustling culinary scene. From exploring the charming Old Town to indulging in the pleasures of the beautiful beaches, Split offers a diverse array of experiences that cater to all interests and preferences.

In addition to the wonders of Split itself, this travel guide will introduce you to the stunning surroundings of the city, from the idyllic islands of Hvar, Brač, and Vis, to the ancient cities of Trogir and Šibenik, as well as the awe-inspiring Krka National Park. Whether you prefer a leisurely day trip or an action-packed adventure, the options for exploration are virtually limitless.

This comprehensive handbook is designed to provide you with all the essential information you'll need to plan your visit to Split, from practical tips on transportation and accommodations to expert recommendations on the best attractions, restaurants, and local experiences. We'll delve into the city's rich history and cultural heritage, uncovering hidden gems and lesser-known attractions, as well as guiding you through the bustling markets, vibrant nightlife, and captivating arts scene.

As you embark on your journey to Split, let this guide be your trusted companion, equipping you with the knowledge and insights needed to make the most of your trip. Whether you're a history buff, a food enthusiast, a beach lover, or an adventure seeker, the magic of Split and its surroundings awaits you, ready to create unforgettable memories that will last a lifetime. So, pack your bags, grab your camera, and get ready to embark on an extraordinary adventure in the enchanting world of Split, Croatia.

Split Travel Guide 2023 And Beyond

CHAPTER ONE

Getting to Know Split

In this chapter, we will introduce you to the vibrant city of Split and provide you with essential information about its history, geography, culture, and climate. As you prepare for your visit, it's essential to understand the background and essence of this captivating destination, which will not only enhance your appreciation for its landmarks and attractions but also help you connect with the local community and their traditions.

History of Split

The history of Split is a fascinating tale that spans over 17 centuries, showcasing its transformation from a small Greek colony to a vibrant, modern city that embraces its rich heritage. To better appreciate Split's historical significance, let's delve into some key moments in the city's timeline.

The area where Split is now situated was initially settled by the Illyrians, an ancient group of tribes that lived in the western Balkans. In the 3rd century BCE, the Greeks founded a colony named Aspálathos (or Spálathos) on the nearby island of Vis, which is believed to be the precursor to modern Split.

The most significant period in Split's history began in 293 CE, when Roman Emperor Diocletian chose the area to build his retirement palace. This sprawling, fortified complex, known as Diocletian's Palace, would become the nucleus around which the city of Split grew. The palace was completed in 305 CE and boasted luxurious living quarters, temples, and military barracks.

Following the fall of the Western Roman Empire, Split became a part of the Byzantine Empire. During the early middle Ages, the city's population increased as residents from the nearby Roman city of Salona sought refuge within the palace walls to escape invasions from Slavic and Avar tribes. Over time, the palace evolved into a bustling urban center, with the original Roman architecture being adapted and repurposed to accommodate the growing population.

In the early 15th century, Split came under the control of the powerful Venetian Republic, which would rule the city for almost 400 years. The Venetians fortified Split and left a lasting impact on its architecture, including the construction of the iconic bell tower of St. Domnius Cathedral.

After the fall of the Venetian Republic, Split came under the rule of the Habsburg Monarchy in 1797. However, this was short-lived, as Napoleon's French Empire took control of the city in 1805. In 1813, the Habsburgs regained control and ruled until the end of World War I.

After the dissolution of the Austro-Hungarian Empire, Split became a part of the Kingdom of Serbs, Croats, and Slovenes, which later became the Kingdom of Yugoslavia. During World War II, Split was occupied by the Axis powers, and the city suffered significant damage from bombing raids.

After World War II, Split became a part of the Socialist Federal Republic of Yugoslavia. During this time, the city experienced rapid industrialization and urbanization. In 1991, Croatia declared independence from Yugoslavia, leading to the Croatian War of Independence. Although Split was not directly affected by the fighting, the city became a vital center for refugees and the Croatian military.

Today, Split is the second-largest city in Croatia and a thriving tourist destination, known for its well-preserved ancient architecture and vibrant modern culture. The city's rich history is evident in its stunning landmarks, making it a fascinating place to explore for history enthusiasts and casual visitors alike.

Geography

Split is located in the Dalmatian region of Croatia, along the eastern shores of the Adriatic Sea. The city covers an area of approximately 79.38 square kilometers (30.65 square miles) and is nestled between the Mosor and Kozjak mountain ranges to the east and the Adriatic Sea to the west. Its coastal location and surrounding mountains create a unique, picturesque setting that draws visitors from around the world.

Split's position on the Adriatic coast has played a significant role in its history and development. The city's natural harbor made it an important strategic and trading center in ancient times and has contributed to its maritime tradition and culture. Today, the harbor serves as a gateway to numerous islands and coastal destinations in the region, making Split an ideal base for exploring the Dalmatian coast.

The city's terrain is characterized by a mix of coastal lowlands and rugged hills. The coastal area features sandy and pebble beaches, as well as rocky cliffs, while the inland regions are marked by forests, karst formations, and agricultural lands. Split's urban area has expanded over time, gradually stretching beyond the confines of Diocletian's Palace and the old town to encompass modern residential and commercial districts.

Split's climate is typical of the Mediterranean, characterized by hot, dry summers and mild, wet winters. The coastal location and surrounding mountains have a significant influence on the city's weather patterns, with the mountains providing some protection from cold continental winds. This results in a pleasant, temperate climate that attracts visitors throughout the year.

Split's geography is characterized by its stunning coastal location, picturesque mountainous surroundings, and pleasant Mediterranean climate. These features have not only shaped the city's history but also contribute to its charm and appeal as a tourist destination.

People and Culture

The people of Split, known as Splicani, are known for their warm and hospitable nature, making visitors feel welcome and at home. The city has a population of approximately 178,000 people, making it the second-largest city in Croatia. Split is a melting pot of various cultures and influences, with a rich history that spans over 17 centuries.

Split's culture is deeply rooted in its history, which dates back to Roman times when Emperor Diocletian built his palace in the city. This ancient heritage is still evident in the city's architecture, language, and customs. The people of Split have a strong connection to their past, which is evident in the way they have preserved their historical sites and embraced their cultural traditions.

The official language of Split is Croatian, which is a South Slavic language. However, many people in the city also speak English, especially those in the tourism and hospitality industries. Due to its coastal location and history as a trading port, Split has been influenced by various cultures, including Italian, Austrian,

Hungarian, and Ottoman. This has resulted in a unique blend of Mediterranean and Central European influences that can be observed in the city's architecture, cuisine, and traditions.

The people of Split are known for their love of sports, particularly soccer and basketball. The city is home to the popular soccer club, Hajduk Split, which has a passionate fan base and a storied history. In addition to soccer, water sports such as sailing, rowing, and swimming are also popular in the city, thanks to its coastal location.

Split has a vibrant arts and cultural scene, with numerous galleries, museums, and theaters showcasing the works of local and international artists. The city is also known for its lively festivals, such as the Split Summer Festival, which features various cultural events, including music, theater, and dance performances.

Cuisine in Split is heavily influenced by its Mediterranean location, with an emphasis on fresh seafood, olive oil, and local produce. Traditional dishes such as pasticada (a slow-cooked beef dish), soparnik (a savory pie filled with Swiss chard), and fritule (a sweet fried doughnut) are popular among locals and visitors alike.

The people and culture of Split are characterized by a rich history, a blend of Mediterranean and Central European influences, a strong connection to sports, a vibrant arts scene, and delicious local cuisine. This unique combination makes Split an exciting and captivating destination for travelers.

Climate

Split has a Mediterranean climate with mild, rainy winters and hot, dry summers. The average temperature in the summer months (June to August) is around 27°C (81°F), while the winter months (December to February) have an average temperature of around 9°C (48°F). The city receives most of its rainfall in the winter months, with an average of 10-12 rainy days per month. The best time to visit Split is from April to October, when the weather is warm and sunny. However, visitors should be prepared for occasional rain showers even during these months.

By gaining a deeper understanding of Split's history, geography, culture, and climate, you'll be better equipped to plan and enjoy a memorable trip. The knowledge you acquire in this chapter will serve as a foundation for your journey as you explore the wonders of Split and its surroundings, enriching your experience and creating a lasting connection with this extraordinary destination.

CHAPTER TWO

Top Sights and Attractions

In this chapter, we will explore the must-see sights and attractions in Split, Croatia, and its surroundings. From ancient Roman ruins and historic landmarks to stunning beaches and picturesque islands, these destinations showcase the best that Split has to offer. We will provide a brief overview of each attraction, along with essential information to help you plan your visit.

Diocletian's Palace

Diocletian's Palace, constructed in the 4th century AD, is a massive ancient Roman palace complex that forms the heart of Split's old town. Built by Emperor Diocletian as his retirement residence, the palace complex has been remarkably well-preserved and is now a UNESCO World Heritage site. The palace is an outstanding example of Roman architecture and urban planning, with a unique blend of military fortress, imperial residence, and fortified city.

The palace covers an area of approximately 31,000 square meters (7.7 acres) and is surrounded by thick walls and four gates: the

Golden Gate (north), the Silver Gate (east), the Iron Gate (west), and the Bronze Gate (south). The palace's layout follows a typical Roman military camp plan, with two main streets (cardo and decumanus) intersecting at the central square, the Peristyle.

Peristyle: This grand central square, surrounded by columns and arches, was once the ceremonial entrance to the imperial apartments. Today, it is a lively public space where locals and visitors gather to enjoy performances, sip coffee, or marvel at the impressive architecture.

Mausoleum of Diocletian (Cathedral of Saint Domnius): Originally built as the final resting place for Emperor Diocletian, the mausoleum was later converted into a cathedral dedicated to Saint Domnius, Split's patron saint. The cathedral showcases a harmonious blend of ancient Roman and Romanesque architecture. Don't miss the intricately carved wooden doors, crafted by Andrija Buvina in the 13th century, depicting scenes from the life of Christ.

Bell Tower of Saint Domnius: The cathedral's bell tower stands 57 meters (187 feet) tall and offers breathtaking panoramic views of Split and the surrounding area. The climb up the tower can be challenging, but the reward is well worth the effort.

Temple of Jupiter: This small temple, dedicated to the Roman god Jupiter, is situated to the west of the Peristyle. The temple's interior features a vaulted ceiling, intricate stone carvings, and a statue of Saint John the Baptist.

Substructures (Basements): The palace's substructures, or basements, are an impressive network of halls and corridors that once supported the upper residential floors. Today, they house various exhibitions, souvenir shops, and occasionally host cultural events.

Visiting Diocletian's Palace: The palace grounds are open 24 hours a day and are free to explore. However, certain attractions within the palace, such as the Cathedral of Saint Domnius, the bell tower, and the substructures, require admission fees. Hours of operation for these attractions may vary by season, so it is advisable to check their schedules before visiting.

When exploring Diocletian's Palace, take the time to wander through the maze-like streets, soak in the atmosphere, and discover hidden squares, courtyards, and shops. This ancient complex offers a fascinating glimpse into Split's history and is an essential part of any visit to the city.

Split Travel Guide 2023 And Beyond

Marjan Hill

Marjan Hill

Marjan Hill, a lush, forested peninsula to the west of Split's city center, is often referred to as the "lungs of the city." It is a popular recreational area for both locals and tourists, offering a peaceful escape from the bustling streets of Split. With its winding paths, beautiful vistas, and historical sites, Marjan Hill provides visitors with a unique combination of nature, culture, and leisure.

Key Features and Activities:

Panoramic Views: Marjan Hill offers stunning panoramic views of Split and the Adriatic Sea from various vantage points. The best views can be found at the hill's summit, marked by a large stone cross, which can be reached by hiking or cycling up the hill.

Beaches: The Marjan peninsula is home to several picturesque beaches, such as Bene, Kasjuni, and Jezinac. These pebble and sand beaches offer crystal-clear waters, making them ideal spots for swimming, sunbathing, or enjoying water sports.

Hiking and Cycling Trails: Marjan Hill is crisscrossed by numerous walking and cycling trails, suitable for various fitness levels. These trails meander through the dense pine forest, offering a refreshing and invigorating experience. Bikes can be rented at various locations near the entrance to Marjan Forest Park.

Split Travel Guide 2023 And Beyond

Historic Churches and Hermitages: Marjan Hill is dotted with small historic churches and hermitages, some dating back to the 13th century. Notable examples include the Church of St. Nicholas, the Church of St. Jerome, and the Church of Our Lady of Seven Sorrows. These religious sites provide an interesting insight into the history and culture of the region.

Recreational Facilities: Marjan Hill offers various recreational facilities, including tennis courts, a jogging track, playgrounds, and a small zoo. The hill is also home to the Split Vidilica, an open-air cafe with a panoramic terrace, where visitors can enjoy refreshments while taking in the breathtaking views.

Visiting Marjan Hill: Marjan Hill is open 24 hours a day and is free to enter. The easiest way to access the hill is by walking or cycling from the city center towards the Marjan Forest Park entrance. Public buses also serve the area, with bus number 12 being the most convenient option. It is advisable to wear comfortable shoes and bring water, especially during the hot summer months, as there are limited facilities available on the hill.

Marjan Hill is an ideal destination for those looking to combine outdoor activities with cultural experiences, all set against the backdrop of Split's stunning coastal landscape. Whether you're interested in hiking, cycling, or simply relaxing on a beach, Marjan Hill offers a refreshing retreat from the city's hustle and bustle.

Riva Promenade

The Riva Promenade, also known as the Split waterfront, is the city's vibrant social hub and a favorite spot for both locals and tourists. This picturesque seafront promenade stretches along the southern edge of the historic Diocletian's Palace and the old town, providing a lively and charming atmosphere that captures the essence of Split's Mediterranean lifestyle.

Key Features and Activities:

Strolling and People-Watching: The Riva Promenade is the perfect place to enjoy a leisurely walk while admiring the stunning harbor views, historic buildings, and palm tree-lined esplanade. With plenty of benches and shaded areas, it's also a great spot for people-watching and soaking in the lively atmosphere.

Cafes, Restaurants, and Bars: The Riva is lined with numerous cafes, restaurants, and bars, offering a wide variety of food and drink options. From casual cafes serving traditional Croatian pastries and ice cream to elegant seafood restaurants and trendy cocktail bars, there's something for everyone on the Riva.

Souvenir and Craft Stalls: Along the promenade, you'll find several souvenir and craft stalls where you can browse and shop for unique gifts, handmade items, and local products. These stalls offer a great opportunity to pick up a memento of your visit to Split.

Events and Performances: The Riva Promenade frequently hosts various events and performances, ranging from concerts and street performers to art exhibitions and cultural festivals. During the summer months, the promenade comes alive with music, dance, and entertainment, adding to its lively ambiance.

Prokurative (Republic Square): Located just off the western end of the Riva Promenade, Prokurative, or Republic Square, is a beautiful 19th-century square designed in the Neo-Renaissance style. The square is surrounded by colorful buildings with arcades and often hosts open-air events, concerts, and performances.

Visiting Riva Promenade: The Riva Promenade is open 24 hours a day and is free to access. It is easily reachable by foot from anywhere in Split's city center, as it runs parallel to the southern walls of Diocletian's Palace. The promenade is wheelchair and stroller-friendly, making it accessible to all visitors.

Whether you're starting your day with a morning coffee, savoring a delicious dinner, or unwinding with a late-night drink, the Riva Promenade offers an unforgettable experience that showcases the best of Split's coastal charm and laid-back lifestyle.

Split Travel Guide 2023 And Beyond

Cathedral of Saint Domnius

The Cathedral of Saint Domnius, also known as the Split Cathedral, is one of the most significant and iconic landmarks in the city. This stunning Romanesque cathedral is dedicated to Saint Domnius, the patron saint of Split. It is housed within the ancient mausoleum of Emperor Diocletian, which was built in the 4th century AD. The unique blend of ancient Roman and medieval architecture makes the Cathedral of Saint Domnius a fascinating site to explore.

Key Features and Highlights:

Mausoleum of Diocletian: The Cathedral of Saint Domnius was originally built as the mausoleum for Emperor Diocletian, who was known for his persecution of Christians. After his death, the mausoleum was later converted into a cathedral, dedicated to Saint Domnius, who was martyred during Diocletian's reign. The transformation of the mausoleum into a cathedral is a powerful symbol of the triumph of Christianity over Roman paganism.

Romanesque Architecture: The interior of the cathedral features a harmonious blend of ancient Roman and Romanesque architecture. The original Roman structure is characterized by a circular layout, a dome with a central oculus, and decorative Corinthian columns. The Romanesque elements include the stone altar, the pulpit, and various sculptures and carvings.

Wooden Doors: The cathedral's main entrance is adorned with intricately carved wooden doors created by Croatian sculptor Andrija Buvina in the 13th century. The doors feature 28 scenes from the life of Christ, showcasing Buvina's remarkable craftsmanship and artistic vision.

Bell Tower: The Cathedral's bell tower, standing at 57 meters (187 feet) tall, is one of the most recognizable features of Split's skyline. Visitors can climb the narrow, winding staircase to the top of the tower for spectacular panoramic views of the city, the harbor, and the surrounding islands. The climb can be challenging, but the breathtaking vistas make it well worth the effort.

Treasury: The Cathedral's treasury, located in a separate building next to the main church, houses a valuable collection of religious artifacts, manuscripts, and works of art. Some of the highlights include intricate gold and silver reliquaries, ancient liturgical books, and vestments.

Visiting Cathedral of Saint Domnius: The Cathedral of Saint Domnius is located within the Diocletian's Palace complex in Split's old town. The hours of operation for the cathedral, bell tower, and treasury may vary by season, so it's recommended to check their schedules before visiting. Admission fees apply for entering the cathedral, climbing the bell tower, and accessing the treasury. It is important to dress modestly when visiting the cathedral, as it is an active place of worship.

The Cathedral of Saint Domnius offers a unique insight into Split's rich history and religious heritage. As you explore the ancient Roman structure and marvel at the Romanesque details, you'll gain a deeper appreciation for the architectural and cultural significance of this remarkable site.

The Islands of Hvar and Brač

The islands of Hvar and Brač are two of the most popular and picturesque destinations in the Adriatic Sea. Both islands are part of the Central Dalmatian archipelago and are easily accessible from Split via ferry or catamaran. They offer visitors a delightful combination of stunning landscapes, charming towns, historic sites, and crystal-clear waters, making them the perfect addition to any trip to Split and its surroundings.

Hvar Island

Hvar Town: Hvar Town, the island's main hub, is known for its elegant Venetian-style architecture, vibrant nightlife, and bustling marina. The town's key attractions include the 13th-century Hvar Cathedral, the historic Hvar Fortress, and the main square, Pjaca.

Stari Grad: Stari Grad, the oldest town on the island, boasts a rich history dating back to ancient Greek times. Key sites to visit include Tvrdalj Castle, the Dominican Monastery, and Stari Grad Plain, a UNESCO World Heritage site featuring ancient agricultural landscapes and stone walls.

Beaches and Coves: Hvar Island is renowned for its stunning beaches and secluded coves, such as Dubovica Beach, Palmižana Beach, and Milna Beach. These pristine locations offer excellent opportunities for swimming, sunbathing, and water sports.

Lavender Fields: Hvar is famous for its lavender fields, which are in full bloom during June and July. The island's lavender products, such as essential oils, soaps, and sachets, make for wonderful souvenirs.

Brač Island

Supetar: Supetar, the island's main town, is known for its lovely beaches, charming streets, and historic sites, such as the Supetar Cemetery and the Church of St. Peter.

Bol: Bol is a popular tourist destination famous for its stunning beach, Zlatni Rat (Golden Horn), which is known for its unique shape and turquoise waters. The town also offers several historical sites, including the Dominican Monastery and the Bol Marina.

Vidova Gora: Vidova Gora, the highest peak on Brač and the highest island peak in the Adriatic, offers breathtaking panoramic views of the island, the sea, and the surrounding archipelago. The peak can be reached via hiking or biking trails.

Pustinja Blaca (Blaca Hermitage): This remarkable 16th-century hermitage, nestled within a dramatic cliffside setting, was once home to a community of Glagolitic monks. Visitors can explore the well-preserved monastery complex and its fascinating history.

Visiting Hvar and Brač Islands: Both Hvar and Brač are easily accessible from Split by ferry or catamaran, with multiple daily departures available during the high season. Travel times range from approximately 1 to 2 hours, depending on the destination and the type of vessel. It is recommended to book tickets in advance, especially during the summer months, as demand can be high.

The islands of Hvar and Brač offer a delightful mix of natural beauty, historic charm, and vibrant culture. Whether you're interested in exploring ancient towns, lounging on pristine beaches, or hiking through picturesque landscapes, these islands provide a memorable experience for visitors of all interests and ages.

Mestrovic Gallery

The Mestrovic Gallery, located in Split, is dedicated to the work of Ivan Mestrovic, one of Croatia's most celebrated artists and sculptors. Mestrovic was a prolific artist whose work spans the early 20th century, with many of his pieces reflecting his passion for Croatian history, culture, and mythology. The gallery is housed in a beautiful villa that was once Mestrovic's home and studio, and it offers visitors a unique insight into the life and work of this remarkable artist.

Key Features and Highlights:

Villa Mestrovic: The Mestrovic Gallery is housed in Villa Mestrovic, a stunning villa designed by the artist himself in the 1930s. The villa showcases Mestrovic's architectural prowess, blending traditional Croatian and modernist elements. The villa is surrounded by well-manicured gardens, which feature several of Mestrovic's sculptures, as well as offering stunning views of the Adriatic Sea.

Sculpture Collection: The gallery boasts an extensive collection of Mestrovic's sculptures, with more than 200 works on display. These works are made from a variety of materials, including bronze, marble, and wood, showcasing the artist's diverse skills and techniques. Some of the most famous pieces on display include the "Well of Life," "Psyche," and "History of the Croats."

Drawings and Paintings: In addition to sculptures, the Mestrovic Gallery also features a selection of the artist's drawings and paintings. These works provide a comprehensive overview of Mestrovic's creative evolution, revealing his varied artistic interests and influences.

Personal Artifacts and Memorabilia: The gallery offers a glimpse into Mestrovic's life through a collection of personal artifacts and memorabilia. Visitors can view his original tools, sketches, and personal belongings, providing a deeper understanding of the man behind the art.

The Mestrovic Gallery is located in the Meje neighborhood of Split, approximately 2 km (1.2 miles) from the city center. It can be reached on foot, by bike, or by taking bus number 12. The gallery is open year-round, with varying hours of operation depending on the season. There is an entrance fee, with discounts available for students, seniors, and groups.

Visiting the Mestrovic Gallery offers an unparalleled opportunity to appreciate the work and life of Ivan Mestrovic, one of Croatia's most influential and celebrated artists. The gallery provides a unique and intimate setting to explore his work, allowing visitors to gain a deeper understanding of Mestrovic's artistry and his lasting impact on Croatian culture.

By exploring these top sights and attractions, you will gain a deep appreciation for the rich history, natural beauty, and vibrant culture of Split and its surroundings. Whether you're interested in ancient architecture, stunning vistas, or sun-soaked beaches, Split offers unforgettable experiences for every type of traveler. Use this chapter as your guide to plan your visit and make the most of your time in this remarkable city.

Split Travel Guide 2023 And Beyond

Map Of Top Sight And Attraction

Borislav Blagoje

CHAPTER THREE

Food and Drink

In this chapter, we delve into the culinary delights that await visitors in Split and its surroundings. The city's gastronomic offerings are deeply rooted in the Mediterranean tradition, with an emphasis on fresh, locally sourced ingredients such as seafood, olive oil, and seasonal produce. As you explore the food and drink scene in Split, you'll encounter a diverse range of flavors and dishes that reflect the city's rich cultural heritage.

Traditional Dalmatian Cuisine

Dalmatian cuisine is deeply rooted in the Mediterranean tradition, characterized by its emphasis on fresh, locally sourced ingredients and simple, yet flavorful dishes. The region's coastal location means that seafood plays a significant role in the local diet, while olive oil, seasonal produce, and aromatic herbs are also essential components. As you explore the culinary offerings of Split and its surroundings, you'll encounter a variety of traditional Dalmatian dishes that showcase the region's rich gastronomic heritage.

Here are some of the key dishes and ingredients:

Peka

Peka is a traditional Dalmatian dish that involves cooking meat, seafood, or vegetables under a bell-shaped dome, or "ispod čripnje." The food is typically placed in a shallow pan, covered with the dome, and cooked slowly over hot coals. Popular variations include octopus, lamb, or veal peka, all of which are often accompanied by potatoes and other vegetables.

Pašticada

Pašticada is a slow-cooked beef dish that's considered a staple of Dalmatian cuisine. The meat is marinated in vinegar and red wine, then braised with onions, carrots, and other vegetables in a rich sauce made from tomatoes, prunes, and a variety of herbs and spices. Pašticada is typically served with homemade gnocchi or pasta.

Crni Rižot (Black Risotto)

Crni rižot, or black risotto, is a popular seafood dish made with Arborio rice, squid, and squid ink, which gives the dish its distinctive black color. Additional ingredients often include garlic, onion, white wine, and a variety of herbs such as parsley and bay leaves. Crni rižot is known for its rich, briny flavors and creamy texture.

Grilled Fish and Seafood

Freshly caught fish and seafood are essential components of Dalmatian cuisine. Grilled fish, such as sea bass, gilt-head bream, and sardines, are commonly served at local restaurants, often accompanied by a simple side dish of Swiss chard and potatoes. Other popular seafood dishes include grilled squid, shrimp, and mussels prepared "na buzaru" (cooked in a tomato, garlic, and white wine sauce).

Soparnik

Soparnik is a traditional Dalmatian savory pastry made from a thin, unleavened dough filled with Swiss chard, onions, and parsley. The pastry is typically baked on a hearth and drizzled with olive oil and crushed garlic before being cut into small squares. Soparnik has been recognized as part of Croatia's intangible cultural heritage.

Olive Oil and Herbs

Olive oil is a cornerstone of Dalmatian cuisine, used for cooking, dressing salads, and drizzling over dishes. The region is known for producing high-quality extra virgin olive oil, which has a fruity, slightly peppery taste. Aromatic herbs like rosemary, sage, basil, and lavender also play a significant role in the local cuisine, adding depth and flavor to various dishes.

By sampling traditional Dalmatian dishes and ingredients, you'll gain a deeper appreciation for the region's culinary heritage and the simple, yet flavorful cuisine that defines the area. Whether you're dining at a local konoba or trying your hand at cooking these dishes yourself, the flavors of Dalmatian cuisine are sure to leave a lasting impression on your taste buds.

Dining in Split

Split offers a diverse range of dining options, from casual konobas (traditional Croatian taverns) and pizzerias to fine dining establishments and seafood restaurants. The city's culinary scene is heavily influenced by its Mediterranean surroundings, featuring an abundance of fresh seafood, seasonal produce, and local ingredients. As you explore Split's dining landscape, you'll find a variety of delicious dishes and eateries to suit every taste and budget.

Key Dining Options and Recommendations:

Konobas: Konobas are traditional Croatian taverns that serve local and regional dishes in a cozy, rustic setting. These establishments often offer great value for money and provide an authentic dining experience. Some popular konobas in Split include Konoba Matejuška, Konoba Hvaranin, and Konoba Kod Joze.

Seafood Restaurants: Given its coastal location, Split is home to numerous seafood restaurants that serve fresh, locally-sourced fish and shellfish. For a memorable seafood experience, consider visiting restaurants such as Nostromo, Sperun, or Zrno Soli.

Fine Dining: Split also boasts several fine dining establishments, where you can enjoy gourmet cuisine and an upscale atmosphere. If you're looking for a more refined dining experience, try restaurants like Restaurant Dvor, Kadena, or Villa Spiza.

Pizzerias: Italian influence is evident in Split's culinary scene, with many pizzerias offering delicious, wood-fired pizzas. Some popular pizzeria options include Bokamorra Pizzaurant & Cocktails, Pizzeria Galija, and Pizzeria Gust.

Street Food and Fast Food: For a quick and budget-friendly meal, Split offers numerous street food and fast food options, such as "burek" (a savory filled pastry), "ćevapi" (grilled meat sausages), and sandwiches. You can find these at various bakeries, fast food joints, and street food stalls throughout the city. Some popular spots include Kantun Paulina, Fast Food Sandra, and To Je Tako.

Vegetarian and Vegan Options: While traditional Dalmatian cuisine is often meat and seafood-heavy, there are several vegetarian and vegan-friendly restaurants in Split. These eateries offer plant-based dishes inspired by both local and international flavors. Notable options include Upcafé, Marta's Veggie Fusion, and Artičok.

Cafés and Dessert Spots: For a coffee break or a sweet treat, Split has plenty of charming cafés and dessert spots to choose from. Enjoy pastries, ice cream, and other confections at places like Luka Ice Cream & Cakes, Café Bar Fro, and O'shura.

As you explore the dining scene in Split, you'll be able to savor the flavors of the Mediterranean and discover the city's rich culinary heritage. With a wide variety of dining options and venues, there's something to suit every palate and budget. Don't hesitate to try new dishes and flavors, as this is one of the best ways to truly immerse yourself in the local culture.

Local Markets and Delicacies

Split's local markets and delicacies offer a vibrant and authentic insight into the city's culinary culture. By visiting these bustling markets and sampling local specialties, you'll gain a deeper appreciation for the fresh, seasonal ingredients and flavors that characterize Dalmatian cuisine.

Key Markets and Delicacies in Split:

Green Market (Pazar): The Green Market, or "Pazar," is a lively outdoor market located in the heart of Split, near the eastern walls of Diocletian's Palace. The market offers a wide variety of fresh fruits, vegetables, cheeses, and cured meats, as well as other local products like olive oil, honey, and homemade liqueurs. As you stroll through the colorful stalls, you'll encounter friendly vendors and a lively atmosphere that captures the essence of Split's daily life.

Fish Market (Ribarnica): Located just a short walk from the Green Market, the Fish Market, or "Ribarnica," is a must-visit for seafood lovers. Here, you'll find an array of freshly caught fish and shellfish from the Adriatic Sea, displayed on beds of ice and sold by local fishermen. The market is open daily, with the best selection available in the early morning hours. Even if you're not planning to buy any seafood, the Ribarnica is worth a visit to soak in the bustling atmosphere and admire the day's catch.

Soparnik: Soparnik is a traditional Dalmatian savory pastry made with a thin, unleavened dough filled with Swiss chard, onions, and parsley. This simple yet delicious dish is typically enjoyed as a snack or appetizer and can be found at bakeries, local markets, and some restaurants. Soparnik has been recognized as part of Croatia's intangible cultural heritage, making it a must-try delicacy during your visit to Split.

Fritule: Fritule are small, sweet fried dough balls that are a popular treat in Split and throughout Dalmatia. These bite-sized desserts are typically flavored with lemon or orange zest, raisins, and a splash of rakija (fruit brandy) before being deep-fried and dusted with powdered sugar. You can find fritule at bakeries, street food stalls, and during local festivals and celebrations.

Prosciutto and Cheese: Dalmatian prosciutto, or "pršut," is a delicious, thinly sliced cured ham that's often served as part of a shared appetizer platter. Pair it with "paški sir," a flavorful sheep's milk cheese from the nearby island of Pag, for a true taste of the region. You can find these delicacies at local markets, specialty food shops, and many restaurants in Split.

Rakija: Rakija is a traditional Croatian fruit brandy that comes in a variety of flavors, such as plum, cherry, and fig. This potent spirit is often enjoyed as a digestive or to toast special occasions. Visit a local market or specialty store to purchase a bottle of rakija as a souvenir or sample some at a local bar or restaurant.

By exploring Split's local markets and sampling the city's delicacies, you'll not only enjoy delicious flavors but also gain a deeper understanding of the city's culinary heritage. These experiences provide an authentic taste of Split's food culture and a unique opportunity to connect with the local community.

Croatian Wine and Wineries

Croatia has a long history of winemaking, dating back to ancient times. The country's diverse climate and terroir have given rise to a wide range of grape varieties and wine styles, making it an exciting destination for wine enthusiasts. Split and its surroundings are home to several notable wine regions, including Dalmatia and the islands of Hvar and Brač. As you explore the local wine scene, you'll have the opportunity to sample some of Croatia's finest wines and learn about the unique winemaking traditions of the area.

Key Grape Varieties and Wine Styles:

Plavac Mali: Plavac Mali is the most widely planted red grape variety in Dalmatia and is responsible for some of Croatia's most renowned red wines. This grape produces full-bodied, tannic wines with flavors of dark fruit, black pepper, and Mediterranean herbs. The wines are often aged in oak, which imparts additional complexity and depth.

Pošip: Pošip is a native white grape variety found primarily in Dalmatia, particularly on the island of Korčula. Pošip wines are typically dry, medium to full-bodied, with flavors of citrus, green apple, and almond. They often have a distinct minerality, which reflects the limestone-rich soils of the region.

Grk: Grk is another indigenous white grape variety, grown mainly on the island of Korčula. This grape produces aromatic, medium-bodied wines with flavors of citrus, peach, and Mediterranean herbs. Grk wines are relatively rare due to the grape's limited production, making them a unique treat for wine lovers.

Vugava: Vugava is a white grape variety native to the island of Vis, located off the Dalmatian coast. The wines produced from Vugava are typically dry, with flavors of apricot, honey, and Mediterranean herbs. Vugava wines can be enjoyed young or aged for several years, which can add complexity and richness to the wine.

Visiting Wineries and Wine Bars in Split and Surrounding Areas:

Wineries: There are numerous wineries in the Split region and nearby islands that welcome visitors for tours and tastings. Some notable wineries include Putalj Winery (located in Kaštela, near Split), Stina Winery (on the island of Brač), and Tomic Winery (on the island of Hvar). These wineries offer a unique opportunity to learn about Croatian winemaking traditions, sample local wines, and enjoy the stunning landscapes of the region.

Wine Bars: If you prefer to explore Croatian wines within the city, Split has several wine bars that offer a wide selection of local and international wines. These establishments provide a relaxed atmosphere in which to taste and learn about Croatian wines, often with knowledgeable staff on hand to guide you through the experience. Some popular wine bars in Split include Zinfandel Food & Wine Bar, Paradox Wine & Cheese Bar, and Art of Wine.

Wine Tastings and Tours: For a more in-depth exploration of the local wine scene, consider booking a guided wine tasting or tour. These experiences often include visits to multiple wineries, vineyards, or wine bars, as well as expert guidance on the region's wines and winemaking history. Wine tasting tours can be found through various local tour operators, such as Split Wine Tours or Secret Dalmatia.

By delving into the Croatian wine scene, you'll gain a deeper understanding of the country's winemaking heritage and the unique grape varieties and styles that define the region. Whether you're visiting

By exploring the city's traditional dishes, local markets, wineries, and vibrant nightlife, you'll gain a deeper appreciation for the region's gastronomic heritage and the flavors that make it truly unique.

CHAPTER FOUR

Nightlife and Entertainment

In this chapter, we will explore the nightlife and entertainment options available in Split, Croatia. The city offers a diverse range of experiences, from lively bars and clubs to cultural events and performances, ensuring there's something for everyone. As you plan your evenings in Split, consider the various venues and activities that cater to different tastes and preferences.

Bars and Pubs

Split's lively bar scene offers a wide range of options for visitors looking to enjoy a drink, socialize, and experience the city's vibrant atmosphere. From cozy pubs to trendy cocktail bars, there's something to suit every taste and preference. Here are some notable bars and pubs in Split that you might want to visit during your stay:

To Je Tako: To Je Tako is a popular bar located in the heart of Split's old town. This stylish venue offers a wide selection of local and international beers, wines, and spirits, as well as a variety of craft cocktails. The bar often hosts live music and DJ sets, providing a lively atmosphere for a night out in Split.

Sanctuary Bar: Sanctuary Bar is a cozy pub located near the Riva Promenade. This laid-back spot is known for its friendly staff, extensive beer selection, and inviting atmosphere. With regular live music performances and a diverse range of drinks, Sanctuary Bar is an excellent choice for a relaxed evening with friends.

Ghetto Club: Situated in a charming courtyard within the old town, Ghetto Club is a unique bar and art gallery that attracts a diverse crowd. The venue offers a range of drinks, including local wines and craft beers, as well as regular live music and DJ sets. Ghetto Club's creative atmosphere and eclectic programming make it a must-visit spot for those seeking a more alternative experience.

Leopold's Delicatessen Bar: Leopold's Delicatessen Bar is a cozy spot that specializes in craft beers, fine wines, and gourmet snacks. With its warm atmosphere and knowledgeable staff, Leopold's is the perfect place to unwind and enjoy a leisurely drink while discovering new flavors.

Charlie's Bar: Popular among backpackers and travelers, Charlie's Bar offers a laid-back atmosphere, affordable drinks, and friendly staff. With regular events like pub quizzes and theme nights, this lively spot is a great place to meet fellow travelers and make new friends.

Marvlvs Library Jazz Bar: Marvlvs Library Jazz Bar is a unique venue that combines a love of books, jazz music, and fine drinks. Located within the walls of Diocletian's Palace, this intimate bar offers a sophisticated atmosphere, an extensive wine list, and regular live jazz performances. It's an ideal spot for those seeking a more cultured night out in Split.

Academia Club Ghetto: Academia Club Ghetto is a popular spot for dancing and enjoying a lively night out. With a mix of music styles, including electronic, hip-hop, and reggae, this club attracts a diverse crowd and offers a fun atmosphere for party-goers.

These are just a few examples of the diverse bars and pubs that you can find in Split. As you explore the city, you'll undoubtedly discover many more hidden gems and local favorites that offer a unique glimpse into Split's vibrant nightlife scene.

Clubs and Nightclubs

Split offers a variety of clubs and nightclubs for those looking to dance the night away or enjoy a more energetic night out. From mainstream clubs playing the latest hits to alternative venues showcasing local and international DJs, there's something for everyone. Here are some notable clubs and nightclubs in Split that you might want to visit during your stay:

Central the Club: Central the Club is a popular nightclub in Split, located in the city center. This spacious venue features multiple bars, a large dance floor, and a VIP area, providing an energetic atmosphere for a night of dancing and socializing. With a mix of electronic and mainstream music, Central the Club attracts a diverse crowd of locals and tourists alike.

Kocka: Kocka is an underground club located near the city center, known for its alternative vibe and eclectic programming. The club hosts a variety of events, including live music, DJ sets, and themed parties, catering to a diverse range of musical tastes. With its unique atmosphere and inclusive ethos, Kocka is a favorite among Split's alternative crowd.

Vanilla Club: Vanilla Club is a stylish nightclub situated in the Poljud area, just a short taxi ride from the city center. This upscale venue features a spacious outdoor terrace, multiple bars, and a sleek, modern interior. With a lineup of local and international DJs spinning house, techno, and other electronic music, Vanilla Club attracts a fashionable crowd looking for a sophisticated night out.

Split Travel Guide 2023 And Beyond

Tropic Club Equador: Located on the popular Bacvice beach, Tropic Club Equador offers a unique beach club experience in Split. The club features an outdoor terrace overlooking the sea, as well as an indoor dance floor and multiple bars. With a mix of electronic and mainstream music, Tropic Club Equador is a popular spot for both day and night partying during the summer months.

Zenta Club: Zenta Club is another popular beach club, located on the Firule beach just a short walk from the city center. This open-air club offers stunning views of the sea and surrounding area, creating a picturesque backdrop for a night of dancing and socializing. With a lineup of local and international DJs, Zenta Club provides a lively atmosphere for those looking to enjoy Split's beachside nightlife.

O'Hara Music Club: O'Hara Music Club is a lively venue located near the Marjan Hill, offering a mix of live music, DJ sets, and themed parties. With its spacious outdoor terrace and multiple bars, O'Hara is a popular spot for locals and tourists looking to dance the night away in a relaxed and friendly atmosphere.

These clubs and nightclubs are just a few examples of the vibrant nightlife options available in Split. As you explore the city, you'll likely discover even more venues catering to a variety of tastes and preferences, ensuring that there's something for everyone when it comes to enjoying a night out in Split.

Cultural Events and Performances

Split boasts a rich cultural scene, with numerous events, concerts, and performances taking place throughout the year. The city's historic venues, outdoor spaces, and theaters provide unique settings for a diverse range of artistic experiences. Here are some of the key cultural events and performances you might want to attend during your visit to Split:

Split Summer Festival: The Split Summer Festival is an annual event held during the months of July and August, showcasing a variety of opera, ballet, theater, and music performances. The festival takes place at various venues across the city, including the historic Peristyle Square and the Croatian National Theatre. This long-running cultural event is a highlight of the summer season and provides a unique opportunity to enjoy world-class performances in stunning surroundings.

Croatian National Theatre (HNK Split): The Croatian National Theatre in Split is one of the city's premier cultural institutions, hosting a range of productions throughout the year. The theater's repertoire includes classical plays, contemporary dramas, operas, ballets, and concerts, catering to a wide range of artistic tastes. The beautiful historic building itself, located in the heart of Split, adds to the experience and is worth a visit.

Split Film Festival: The Split Film Festival, also known as the International Festival of New Film, is held annually in September. This week-long event showcases a diverse selection of independent films, documentaries, and experimental cinema from around the world. Screenings take place at various venues across the city, including the Kino Karaman and the Bacvice Open-Air Cinema, providing an immersive experience for film enthusiasts.

Youth Theatre (Kazalište Mladih): The Youth Theatre in Split is dedicated to nurturing young talent and promoting contemporary theater. With a diverse range of productions, including original works and adaptations of classic plays, the theater provides a platform for emerging artists and directors. The intimate venue, located near the Riva Promenade, offers a unique opportunity to experience the future of Croatian theater.

Outdoor Concerts and Performances: During the summer months, Split's historic squares and outdoor spaces often host a variety of concerts and performances. From classical music ensembles to local bands and dance troupes, these events offer a unique way to experience the city's vibrant cultural scene. Keep an eye out for event listings and posters around the city to discover upcoming performances during your stay.

Art Galleries and Exhibitions: Split is home to several art galleries and exhibition spaces, showcasing the work of both local and international artists. The Gallery of Fine Arts, located near the city center, features a permanent collection of Croatian art, as well as rotating exhibitions. Smaller galleries, such as the Mestrovic Gallery and the Jaman Art Gallery, provide a more intimate setting to explore the city's contemporary art scene.

These cultural events and performances represent just a glimpse of the diverse artistic experiences available in Split. As you explore the city, you'll likely encounter even more opportunities to immerse yourself in the local culture and enjoy a memorable evening of entertainment.

Live Music

Live music is an integral part of Split's nightlife, with a variety of venues hosting performances by local and international artists throughout the year. From intimate jazz bars to lively pubs and open-air stages, there's a wide range of options for music lovers in the city. Here are some notable live music venues and events in Split that you might want to check out during your stay:

Marvlvs Library Jazz Bar: Marvlvs Library Jazz Bar is a unique venue that combines a love of books, jazz music, and fine drinks. Located within the walls of Diocletian's Palace, this intimate bar offers a sophisticated atmosphere, an extensive wine list, and regular live jazz performances. It's an ideal spot for those seeking a more cultured night out in Split.

Ghetto Club: Situated in a charming courtyard within the old town, Ghetto Club is a unique bar and art gallery that attracts a diverse crowd. The venue offers a range of drinks, including local wines and craft beers, as well as regular live music and DJ sets. Ghetto Club's creative atmosphere and eclectic programming make it a must-visit spot for those seeking a more alternative experience.

Sanctuary Bar: Sanctuary Bar is a cozy pub located near the Riva Promenade. This laid-back spot is known for its friendly staff, extensive beer selection, and inviting atmosphere. With regular live music performances and a diverse range of drinks, Sanctuary Bar is an excellent choice for a relaxed evening with friends.

Riva Promenade: The Riva Promenade, located along Split's waterfront, is a popular spot for both locals and tourists. During the summer months, you can often find live music performances taking place on the promenade, with musicians and bands setting up to entertain the crowds. These impromptu concerts provide a lively and enjoyable atmosphere, perfect for a warm evening stroll.

Peristyle Square: Peristyle Square is the central square within Diocletian's Palace, offering a unique setting for live music performances. Throughout the year, you can often find local musicians and bands performing in the square, surrounded by the palace's historic architecture. These performances are particularly magical during the summer months when the square is lit up and filled with people enjoying the music.

To Je Tako: To Je Tako is a popular bar located in the heart of Split's old town. This stylish venue offers a wide selection of local and international beers, wines, and spirits, as well as a variety of craft cocktails. The bar often hosts live music and DJ sets, providing a lively atmosphere for a night out in Split.

Split Summer Festival: The Split Summer Festival, held during July and August, features a variety of musical performances in addition to its theater, opera, and ballet events. Concerts take place at various venues across the city, showcasing local and international artists spanning a range of genres. Attending a live music performance during the festival is a great way to experience the city's vibrant cultural scene.

These live music venues and events in Split offer a diverse range of experiences for music lovers, from intimate jazz performances to lively open-air concerts. As you explore the city, you'll likely discover even more opportunities to enjoy live music and immerse yourself in Split's thriving nightlife scene.

Outdoor Cinemas

Outdoor cinemas provide a unique and enjoyable way to experience movies under the stars during the warm summer months in Split. These open-air venues offer a mix of classic films, recent releases, and international cinema, making for a memorable evening of entertainment. Here are some notable outdoor cinemas in Split that you might want to visit during your stay:

Bacvice Open-Air Cinema (Kino Bačvice): Bacvice Open-Air Cinema is a popular summertime venue, located near the famous Bacvice beach. This outdoor cinema offers a diverse program of films, including Hollywood blockbusters, independent productions, and

Croatian movies. With comfortable seating, a relaxed atmosphere, and the warm Mediterranean breeze, Kino Bačvice provides an unforgettable movie-watching experience in Split.

Old City Open-Air Cinema (Kino Stari Grad): Kino Stari Grad is another open-air cinema located in the heart of Split's old town. This picturesque venue screens a range of classic and contemporary films, surrounded by the city's historic architecture. With its unique setting and intimate atmosphere, Kino Stari Grad offers a one-of-a-kind movie night under the stars.

Marjan Open-Air Cinema (Kino Marjan): Located on the slopes of Marjan Hill, Kino Marjan is an open-air cinema that offers stunning views of the city and the sea. During the summer months, the cinema screens a variety of films, including recent releases and international cinema. The elevated location and panoramic vistas make Kino Marjan an exceptional venue for an outdoor movie night in Split.

Film Festivals: In addition to the regular open-air cinemas, Split hosts several film festivals throughout the year, which often include outdoor screenings. The Split Film Festival, held in September, showcases a diverse selection of independent films, documentaries, and experimental cinema from around the world.

Screenings take place at various venues across the city, including outdoor cinemas like Kino Bačvice and Kino Stari Grad.

These outdoor cinemas and film events in Split offer a unique way to enjoy movies in the city's picturesque surroundings. As you explore the city during the summer months, be sure to check the local listings and event schedules to discover upcoming outdoor screenings and make the most of your time in Split.

Sports Bars

Split has a strong sporting culture, with football, basketball, and water sports being particularly popular among locals. As a result, the city offers a variety of sports bars where fans can gather to watch live games, enjoy a drink, and socialize. Here are some notable sports bars in Split that you might want to visit during your stay:

Caffe Bar Žbirac: Caffe Bar Žbirac is a popular sports bar located near the famous Bacvice beach. With multiple screens broadcasting various sports events, this lively venue offers a relaxed atmosphere, a wide selection of drinks, and friendly staff. Žbirac is an ideal spot to watch a game while enjoying the beachside location.

Charlie's Bar: Charlie's Bar is a cozy pub situated in the heart of Split's old town. This welcoming venue offers a range of local and international beers, as well as a variety of spirits and cocktails. With multiple screens showing live sports events, Charlie's Bar is a great option for those seeking a more intimate sports bar experience.

Fabrique Pub: Fabrique Pub is a spacious sports bar located in the city center, offering a wide selection of beers, wines, and spirits. With numerous screens broadcasting live sports events, comfortable seating, and a lively atmosphere, Fabrique Pub is an excellent choice for watching a game with friends or fellow sports enthusiasts.

Fidel Gastro Pub: Fidel Gastro Pub is a stylish venue located near the Riva Promenade. This modern pub offers a diverse menu of craft beers, cocktails, and wines, as well as a selection of gourmet pub food. With multiple screens showing live sports events and a relaxed atmosphere, Fidel Gastro Pub is a great option for a more upscale sports bar experience.

Sanctuary Bar: As mentioned earlier, Sanctuary Bar is a cozy pub near the Riva Promenade, known for its friendly staff and extensive beer selection. In addition to its welcoming atmosphere, the bar also features multiple screens for watching live sports events, making it a popular choice among sports fans in Split.

Caffe Bar Tropic: Caffe Bar Tropic is a laid-back sports bar situated near the Marjan Hill. This venue offers a range of beers, wines, and spirits, as well as comfortable seating and multiple screens for watching live sports events. With its relaxed atmosphere and picturesque location, Tropic is an ideal spot to enjoy a game while taking in the stunning views of Split.

These sports bars in Split offer a variety of atmospheres and experiences for watching live sports events, from cozy pubs to modern venues. As you explore the city, you'll likely discover even more options to enjoy a game and immerse yourself in the local sports culture.

As you explore the nightlife and entertainment options in Split, you'll discover a vibrant and diverse scene that caters to various tastes and preferences. From lively bars and clubs to cultural events and performances, there's no shortage of ways to enjoy an evening in this beautiful Croatian city.

Borislav Blagoje

CHAPTER FIVE

Accommodation

In this Chapter, we provide an overview of the various accommodation options available in Split, Croatia, and its surroundings. From luxury hotels to budget-friendly hostels, private apartments to cozy guesthouses, Split offers a range of options to suit every traveler's preferences and budget. In this chapter, we'll explore some of the top accommodation choices in the city, as well as tips for finding the perfect place to stay during your visit.

Luxury Hotels

Split offers a selection of luxury hotels that cater to travelers seeking high-end accommodations, exceptional service, and top-notch amenities. These hotels often feature fine dining restaurants, spa facilities, and prime locations, ensuring a comfortable and memorable stay. Here are some of the top luxury hotels in Split:

Le Méridien Lav: Le Méridien Lav is a stunning 5-star hotel located in Podstrana, about 8 km south of Split's city center. Situated along the Adriatic coastline, the hotel offers breathtaking sea views, stylish rooms, and suites with modern amenities. Guests can enjoy the hotel's private beach, a luxurious spa and wellness center, several fine dining restaurants, and an array of recreational facilities, including tennis courts and a marina.

Hotel Park: Hotel Park is a historic 5-star hotel located in the elite Bacvice neighborhood, just a short walk from the famous Bacvice beach and the city center. This elegant hotel features luxurious rooms and suites, an outdoor swimming pool, a fine dining restaurant, and a spa and wellness center. With its prime location, impeccable service, and refined atmosphere, Hotel Park provides an unforgettable stay in Split.

Hotel Vestibul Palace: Hotel Vestibul Palace is a boutique 5-star hotel situated within the walls of Diocletian's Palace, in the heart of Split's old town. This unique hotel seamlessly blends contemporary design with the historic architecture of the palace. The hotel offers a selection of luxurious rooms and suites, a fine dining restaurant, and personalized service, ensuring a memorable experience in the heart of Split's historic center.

Hotel Atrium: Hotel Atrium is a modern 5-star hotel located within walking distance of Split's city center and main attractions. The hotel features stylish rooms and suites, a fine dining restaurant, a rooftop terrace with stunning city views, and a spa and wellness center. With its convenient location and high-quality amenities, Hotel Atrium is an excellent choice for a luxurious stay in Split.

Radisson Blu Resort & Spa Split: Radisson Blu Resort & Spa is a contemporary 5-star hotel situated along the Adriatic coast, about 3 km from Split's city center. The hotel offers spacious rooms and suites with sea views, a private beach, an extensive spa and wellness center, and several dining options, including a fine dining restaurant. The hotel's prime beachfront location and upscale amenities make it an ideal choice for a relaxing and luxurious stay in Split.

Cornaro Hotel: Cornaro Hotel is a 4-star boutique hotel located in the heart of Split, just a short walk from Diocletian's Palace and the Riva Promenade. This elegant hotel offers a range of luxurious rooms and suites, a rooftop terrace with panoramic city views, a fine dining restaurant, and a spa and wellness center. With its central location and high-quality amenities, Cornaro Hotel provides a comfortable and stylish base for exploring Split.

These luxury hotels in Split offer a range of upscale accommodations, exceptional service, and top-notch amenities, ensuring a comfortable and memorable stay in this beautiful city. Whether you're seeking a beachfront resort, a historic boutique hotel, or a modern city retreat, Split's luxury hotels cater to a variety of preferences and provide an unforgettable experience for discerning travelers.

For travelers seeking a luxurious stay, Split boasts a selection of high-end hotels that offer exceptional service, elegant rooms, and top-notch amenities. Some of the top luxury hotels in the city include Le Méridien Lav, Hotel Park, and Hotel Vestibul Palace. These hotels often feature fine dining restaurants, spa facilities, and prime locations, ensuring a comfortable and memorable stay.

Mid-Range Hotels

For travelers seeking a balance between quality and affordability, mid-range hotels in Split offer comfortable rooms, convenient locations, and a range of amenities at a reasonable price. Here are some popular mid-range hotels in the city that provide a comfortable base for exploring Split without breaking the bank:

Hotel Luxe: Hotel Luxe is a stylish 4-star hotel located within walking distance of Split's city center, Diocletian's Palace, and the

Riva Promenade. The hotel features contemporary rooms with modern amenities, a spa and wellness center, a small fitness area, and a buffet breakfast. Its prime location and excellent service make Hotel Luxe a popular choice among travelers.

Hotel Cvita: Hotel Cvita is a 4-star hotel located in a peaceful residential area, just a short drive or bus ride from Split's city center. This modern hotel offers spacious rooms with elegant furnishings, an outdoor swimming pool, a fitness center, and a restaurant serving local and international cuisine. With its serene atmosphere and convenient location, Hotel Cvita provides a comfortable and relaxing stay in Split.

Hotel Marul: Hotel Marul is a boutique 4-star hotel located within walking distance of Diocletian's Palace, the Riva Promenade, and Marjan Hill. This charming hotel features individually decorated rooms with modern amenities, a lovely garden terrace, and a buffet breakfast. The hotel's friendly staff and central location make it an excellent choice for exploring Split.

Hotel Slavija: Hotel Slavija is a 3-star hotel situated within the walls of Diocletian's Palace, offering a unique accommodation experience in the heart of Split's historic center. The hotel provides comfortable rooms with modern amenities, a rooftop terrace with stunning views of the city, and a buffet breakfast. Its prime location and affordable rates make Hotel Slavija a popular choice among travelers.

Hotel Ora: Hotel Ora is a 4-star hotel located in the Poljud neighborhood, just a short walk from the Poljud Stadium and a quick bus ride from the city center. This contemporary hotel offers spacious rooms with modern amenities, an on-site restaurant serving Mediterranean cuisine, and a fitness center. Hotel Ora's convenient location and excellent service make it a great option for a comfortable stay in Split.

Hotel As: Hotel As is a 3-star hotel located in the residential area of Znjan, about 3 km from Split's city center. This modern hotel offers comfortable rooms with sea views, an on-site restaurant, and a lovely terrace overlooking the Adriatic Sea. Its peaceful atmosphere and proximity to the beach make Hotel As a popular choice for travelers seeking a quieter stay in Split.

These mid-range hotels in Split offer a variety of accommodations and amenities at reasonable prices, providing a comfortable base for exploring the city without stretching your budget. With options ranging from boutique hotels in the city center to peaceful retreats near the beach, mid-range hotels in Split cater to a variety of preferences and provide an enjoyable stay for travelers of all types.

Budget Hotels and Hostels

For travelers on a tight budget, Split offers several budget hotels and hostels that provide basic amenities and a friendly atmosphere. These affordable accommodations allow you to experience Split while meeting fellow travelers from around the world. Here are some of the top budget hotels and hostels in the city:

Hotel Dujam: Hotel Dujam is a 2-star hotel located within walking distance of Split's city center and main attractions. This budget-friendly hotel offers basic but comfortable rooms with private bathrooms, a buffet breakfast, and a 24-hour reception. With its convenient location and affordable rates, Hotel Dujam is an excellent choice for travelers seeking a no-frills stay in Split.

Design Hostel Goli & Bosi: Design Hostel Goli & Bosi is a modern and stylish hostel located in the heart of Split's old town, just a short walk from Diocletian's Palace and the Riva Promenade. The hostel offers a variety of dormitory rooms and private rooms, a shared kitchen and common areas, and a friendly and helpful staff. Its prime location, contemporary design, and affordable rates make Goli & Bosi a popular choice among budget travelers.

Tchaikovsky Hostel: Tchaikovsky Hostel is a charming and cozy hostel situated within walking distance of Split's main attractions. This boutique-style hostel offers a range of dormitory rooms and private rooms, a shared kitchen and lounge area, and a friendly and welcoming atmosphere. The hostel's unique music-themed decor, attentive staff, and affordable rates make it an excellent option for budget-conscious travelers.

Old Town Hostel: Old Town Hostel is a budget-friendly hostel located in the heart of Split's historic center, just steps from Diocletian's Palace. The hostel offers a variety of dormitory rooms and private rooms, a shared kitchen and common areas, and a fun and social atmosphere. With its central location, friendly staff, and affordable rates, Old Town Hostel is a popular choice among backpackers and budget travelers.

Hostel Split Backpackers: Hostel Split Backpackers is a vibrant and social hostel located within walking distance of the city center and the main bus and train stations. The hostel offers dormitory rooms and private rooms, a shared kitchen and common areas, and a lively atmosphere with organized events and activities. Its convenient location and budget-friendly rates make Hostel Split Backpackers an excellent choice for travelers seeking a social and affordable stay in Split.

Hostel D&D: Hostel D&D is a small and cozy hostel located just a short walk from Split's city center and main attractions. This budget-friendly hostel offers dormitory rooms and private rooms, a shared kitchen and lounge area, and a welcoming atmosphere. With its convenient location, attentive staff, and affordable rates, Hostel D&D is a great option for budget travelers seeking a comfortable stay in Split.

These budget hotels and hostels in Split offer a range of affordable accommodations, basic amenities, and friendly atmospheres, providing a cost-effective way to experience the city while meeting fellow travelers. With options ranging from no-frills hotels to vibrant and social hostels, budget accommodations in Split cater to a variety of preferences and provide an enjoyable stay for travelers on a tight budget.

Private Apartments and Vacation Rentals

For travelers who prefer the comforts and privacy of a home away from home, private apartments and vacation rentals are a popular choice in Split. These accommodations allow you to experience the city like a local while enjoying the flexibility to cook your meals and set your schedule. Here are some tips and recommendations for finding the perfect private apartment or vacation rental in Split:

Booking Platforms: Websites like Airbnb, Booking.com, and Vrbo offer a wide range of private apartments and vacation rentals in Split. These platforms allow you to filter your search based on factors such as location, price, and amenities, making it easy to find the perfect accommodation for your needs and preferences.

Types of Accommodations: Private apartments and vacation rentals in Split come in various sizes and styles, from modern studios in the city center to spacious villas with sea views. You can find accommodations that cater to solo travelers, couples, families, or large groups, ensuring a comfortable stay for everyone.

Location: When choosing a private apartment or vacation rental in Split, consider the location based on your interests and itinerary. Staying in the city center or near the Riva Promenade provides easy access to the main attractions, while staying further from the city center can offer a more peaceful and budget-friendly experience. For beach lovers, accommodations in the Bacvice, Znjan, or Podstrana neighborhoods provide easy access to the sea.

Split Travel Guide 2023 And Beyond

Amenities: Private apartments and vacation rentals in Split often come with a range of amenities, such as fully equipped kitchens, air conditioning, Wi-Fi, and laundry facilities. Be sure to check the listing for details on what is included, as amenities can vary between properties.

Reviews: Before booking a private apartment or vacation rental in Split, read reviews from previous guests to get a sense of the quality and atmosphere of the accommodation. Reviews can provide valuable insights into factors such as cleanliness, location, and the responsiveness of the host.

Booking Tips: Book your private apartment or vacation rental well in advance, particularly during the peak tourist season (June to August), as popular options can fill up quickly.

Be sure to communicate with your host before and during your stay. They can often provide valuable tips and recommendations for exploring the local area and making the most of your visit to Split.

By exploring the diverse range of private apartments and vacation rentals available in Split, you can find the perfect home away from home during your visit. These accommodations offer the flexibility, privacy, and comfort that many travelers prefer, providing a unique and memorable experience in this beautiful city.

Guesthouses and Bed & Breakfasts

Guesthouses and bed & breakfasts are an excellent choice for travelers seeking a more personal and intimate experience during their stay in Split. These accommodations typically offer fewer rooms and a homey atmosphere, allowing guests to enjoy a warm and welcoming environment. Here are some tips and recommendations for finding the perfect guesthouse or bed & breakfast in Split:

Booking Platforms: Websites like Booking.com, TripAdvisor, and Expedia offer a wide range of guesthouses and bed & breakfasts in Split. These platforms allow you to filter your search based on factors such as location, price, and amenities, making it easy to find the perfect accommodation for your needs and preferences.

Types of Accommodations: Guesthouses and bed & breakfasts in Split come in various styles, from traditional stone houses in the historic center to modern guesthouses in residential neighborhoods. These accommodations can cater to solo travelers, couples, or families, providing a comfortable stay for a range of guests.

Location: When choosing a guesthouse or bed & breakfast in Split, consider the location based on your interests and itinerary. Staying in the city center or near the Riva Promenade provides easy access to the main attractions, while staying further from the city center can offer a more peaceful and budget-friendly experience. For beach lovers, accommodations in the Bacvice, Znjan, or Podstrana neighborhoods provide easy access to the sea.

Amenities: Guesthouses and bed & breakfasts in Split often come with a range of amenities, such as private bathrooms, air conditioning, Wi-Fi, and sometimes even a shared kitchen or common areas. Many of these accommodations also include breakfast, which can be served in a communal dining area or directly to your room.

Reviews: Before booking a guesthouse or bed & breakfast in Split, read reviews from previous guests to get a sense of the quality and atmosphere of the accommodation. Reviews can provide valuable insights into factors such as cleanliness, location, and the friendliness of the hosts.

Booking Tips: Book your guesthouse or bed & breakfast well in advance, particularly during the peak tourist season (June to August), as popular options can fill up quickly. Reach out to the hosts before and during your stay, as they can often provide valuable tips and recommendations for exploring the local area and making the most of your visit to Split.

By exploring the diverse range of guesthouses and bed & breakfasts available in Split, you can find the perfect accommodation that offers a warm, welcoming, and personal experience during your visit. These accommodations provide a unique and intimate alternative to larger hotels, allowing you to enjoy the hospitality and charm of this beautiful city.

Accommodation Tips

When choosing your accommodation in Split, consider factors such as location, budget, and personal preferences. Staying in the city center or near the Riva Promenade provides easy access to the main attractions, while staying further from the city center can offer a more peaceful and budget-friendly experience.

Choosing the right accommodation for your trip to Split is essential for a comfortable and enjoyable stay. Here are some tips to help you find the perfect place to rest your head after a day of exploring this beautiful city:

Determine Your Priorities: Before booking your accommodation, consider what is most important to you during your stay. This could include factors such as location, budget, amenities, or atmosphere. Knowing your priorities will help you narrow down your options and find the best fit for your needs and preferences.

Research Neighborhoods: Split has a variety of neighborhoods, each with its unique atmosphere and attractions. Research the different areas to determine which one suits your interests and travel style. Some popular neighborhoods include the historic city center, the vibrant Bacvice beach area, and the peaceful residential neighborhoods of Marjan Hill and Znjan.

Read Reviews: Reading reviews from previous guests can provide valuable insights into the quality and atmosphere of an accommodation. Look for consistent feedback about cleanliness, location, service, and any specific features that are important to you.

Book Early: To secure your preferred accommodation, it's a good idea to book early, especially during the peak tourist season (June to August). Early booking can also provide better rates and availability.

Be Flexible with Dates: If you have some flexibility in your travel dates, consider visiting Split during the shoulder seasons (April-May and September-October). Accommodations are often more affordable and less crowded during these periods, allowing you to enjoy a more relaxed stay.

Consider Alternative Accommodations: Depending on your preferences, consider alternative accommodation options such as guesthouses, bed & breakfasts, private apartments, or vacation rentals. These options can provide a unique and memorable experience, often with a more personal touch.

Check for Hidden Fees: Be sure to read the fine print and inquire about any additional fees or charges that may not be included in the listed price. This could include city taxes, cleaning fees, or extra charges for amenities.

Reach Out to Your Hosts: Communicate with your hosts or hotel staff before and during your stay. They can often provide valuable tips and recommendations for exploring the local area, as well as assist with any special requests or concerns.

Be Aware of Cancellation Policies: Before booking your accommodation, review the cancellation policy to ensure it meets your needs. Policies can vary between accommodations, with some offering free cancellation up to a certain date, while others may have stricter, non-refundable terms.

By considering these accommodation tips, you can find the perfect place to stay in Split that suits your preferences, budget, and travel style. With a comfortable and well-chosen base, you'll be well-prepared to enjoy all the beauty and charm that Split has to offer.

By exploring the diverse accommodation options in Split, you can find the perfect place to stay during your visit. In Chapter 6 of the Split Travel Guide 2023, we provide insights and recommendations to help you make an informed decision and ensure a comfortable, enjoyable experience in this beautiful city.

Borislav Blagoje

CHAPTER SIX

Lesser-Known Attractions And Experiences (Hidden Gem)

In this Chapter, we delve into the lesser-known attractions and experiences that make this vibrant city truly special. While Split is famous for its iconic landmarks, such as Diocletian's Palace and Marjan Hill, it also offers a wealth of hidden gems waiting to be discovered by curious travelers. In this chapter, we'll explore some of the off-the-beaten-path locations, local secrets, and unique experiences that will make your visit to Split even more memorable.

Veli Varoš Neighborhood

Veli Varoš is a charming and historic neighborhood in Split, located just west of the city center and the famous Diocletian's Palace. With its narrow cobblestone streets, traditional stone houses, and picturesque surroundings, Veli Varoš offers a glimpse into Split's authentic local life, away from the bustling tourist areas. Here are some highlights and details about the Veli Varoš neighborhood:

History and Architecture: Veli Varoš dates back to the 17th century and is one of the oldest neighborhoods in Split. The area is characterized by its traditional Dalmatian stone houses with red-tiled roofs, narrow streets, and winding alleys. Many of these buildings have been carefully restored, maintaining their historical charm while incorporating modern amenities.

Marjan Hill: Veli Varoš is situated at the foot of Marjan Hill, a lush forest park that offers stunning views of the city, the Adriatic Sea, and the surrounding islands. Marjan Hill is a popular spot for outdoor activities, such as hiking, biking, and rock climbing, as well as for enjoying the tranquil beaches and coves along its shores.

Church of St. Nicholas: One of the neighborhood's most notable landmarks is the Church of St. Nicholas, a small 13th-century church perched on a hill overlooking Veli Varoš. The church's charming exterior and panoramic views of the city make it a popular spot for photography enthusiasts and visitors seeking a peaceful retreat.

Restaurants and Cafés: Veli Varoš is home to a number of local restaurants and cafés where you can sample traditional Dalmatian cuisine, such as grilled fish, pasticada (a slow-cooked beef dish), and soparnik (a savory pie with Swiss chard and onions). The neighborhood's eateries offer a more authentic and relaxed dining experience compared to the tourist-oriented establishments in the city center.

Accommodations: The Veli Varoš neighborhood offers a variety of accommodation options, including guesthouses, bed & breakfasts, and private apartments. Staying in this area allows you to experience the local atmosphere while still being within walking distance of Split's main attractions.

Accessibility: Veli Varoš is easily accessible on foot from Split's city center and main bus station, making it a convenient base for exploring the city and its surroundings. The neighborhood's narrow streets and steep staircases may be challenging for those with mobility issues, so it's essential to consider this when choosing your accommodation.

By visiting the Veli Varoš neighborhood, you can immerse yourself in the authentic charm and history of Split. This picturesque area offers a peaceful retreat from the bustling city center while providing easy access to the main attractions, making it an ideal choice for travelers seeking a more local and genuine experience in Split.

Bene Beach

Bene Beach is a picturesque and tranquil spot located on the northern slopes of Marjan Hill in Split, Croatia. This beautiful pebble beach is surrounded by lush pine forests, providing a serene escape from the city's hustle and bustle. Here are some highlights and details about Bene Beach:

Getting There: To reach Bene Beach, you can either hike or bike through Marjan Forest Park or take a bus (number 12) from the city center. The bus ride takes approximately 15-20 minutes, and the bus stop is conveniently located near the beach. Alternatively, you can also take a taxi or drive, but keep in mind that parking spaces are limited during peak season.

Beach Features: Bene Beach is a pebble beach with crystal-clear waters, making it perfect for swimming and snorkeling. The surrounding pine forest offers natural shade, and there are plenty of spots to relax and sunbathe. Beach chairs and umbrellas are available for rent, providing additional comfort for visitors.

Amenities: Bene Beach offers various amenities, such as changing rooms, showers, and restrooms. There's also a beach bar and a restaurant serving refreshments, snacks, and local dishes. Visitors can rent kayaks, paddleboards, and other water sports equipment to explore the nearby coves and coastline.

Family-Friendly: Bene Beach is an excellent option for families, as it features a children's playground, a small water park, and a dedicated swimming area for kids. The beach's calm waters and relaxed atmosphere make it an ideal spot for families with young children.

Sports and Recreation: In addition to water sports, Bene Beach offers a range of sports facilities, including tennis courts, a basketball court, and a soccer field. Visitors can also enjoy the walking and biking trails that wind through Marjan Forest Park, providing a great opportunity to explore the park's natural beauty and stunning viewpoints.

Nearby Attractions: While visiting Bene Beach, take the opportunity to explore the rest of Marjan Forest Park, which boasts numerous walking and biking trails, historic chapels, and scenic viewpoints. The park also houses the Split Zoo and the Mestrovic Gallery, which showcases the work of Croatian sculptor Ivan Meštrović.

Bene Beach is a charming and peaceful destination that offers a perfect blend of natural beauty, recreational activities, and essential amenities. Its family-friendly atmosphere, pristine waters, and stunning surroundings make it an ideal choice for those seeking a relaxing day at the beach away from Split's more crowded and touristy areas.

Joze Tea House

Jože Tea House, located in the heart of Split's historic city center, is a cozy and charming tea house that offers a wide selection of high-quality teas, as well as coffee, pastries, and light snacks. This hidden gem is a perfect spot for tea enthusiasts or anyone seeking a peaceful retreat from the bustling streets of Split. Here are some highlights and details about Jože Tea House:

Ambiance and Décor: Jože Tea House features a warm and inviting atmosphere, with vintage-inspired furniture, colorful cushions, and an eclectic mix of decorative elements. The cozy interior creates a welcoming space for guests to relax and enjoy their beverages.

Tea Selection: The tea house offers a diverse range of premium loose-leaf teas, including black, green, white, oolong, and herbal varieties. Guests can choose from classic favorites like Earl Grey and Darjeeling, as well as more exotic blends and unique Croatian teas. The knowledgeable staff can guide you through the selection and help you find the perfect tea to suit your taste.

Coffee and Other Beverages: In addition to tea, Jože Tea House serves a variety of coffee beverages, such as espressos, cappuccinos, and lattes. For those looking for a cold and refreshing drink, the tea house also offers freshly squeezed juices and homemade lemonades.

Pastries and Light Snacks: Jože Tea House complements its tea and coffee offerings with a selection of delicious homemade pastries, cakes, and cookies. Light snacks, such as sandwiches and quiches, are also available for those looking for a more substantial bite.

Location: The tea house is conveniently situated in the heart of Split's city center, just a short walk from the Diocletian's Palace and the Riva Promenade. It is tucked away on a quiet side street, providing a peaceful escape from the city's hustle and bustle.

Events and Workshops: Jože Tea House occasionally hosts tea-related events and workshops, offering visitors the opportunity to learn more about tea culture, preparation, and history. Keep an eye on their social media pages for announcements about upcoming events.

Jože Tea House is a delightful and tranquil spot in Split, where you can enjoy a wide range of high-quality teas, coffee, and tasty treats in a relaxed and cozy atmosphere. Whether you are a tea enthusiast or simply in search of a quiet place to unwind, Jože Tea House provides the perfect setting for a memorable and soothing experience in the heart of Split.

The Froggyland Museum

The Froggyland Museum is a quirky and unique attraction located in the heart of Split, Croatia. This one-of-a-kind museum is home to a collection of over 500 taxidermy frogs, each posed in various everyday human scenes, such as playing sports, attending school, or enjoying a night out. Here are some highlights and details about The Froggyland Museum:

The Collection: The Froggyland Museum houses an extensive collection of taxidermy frogs created by Hungarian taxidermist Ferenc Mere between 1910 and 1920. Mere painstakingly preserved and posed each frog by hand, using various techniques to create intricate and lifelike dioramas that showcase the frogs engaged in everyday human activities.

Dioramas and Themes: The museum features 21 dioramas, each depicting a different aspect of human life, such as work, leisure, and family. Visitors can explore scenes of frogs attending school, playing cards, dining at a restaurant, and even getting married. The dioramas' intricate details and creative themes make for a fascinating and entertaining experience.

Educational Value: While The Froggyland Museum is undoubtedly a quirky and amusing attraction, it also provides educational value. The museum showcases the impressive skill and artistry of Ferenc Mere, and it offers insight into early 20th-century taxidermy techniques. The museum also highlights the importance of preserving and appreciating our natural world.

Location and Accessibility: The Froggyland Museum is conveniently located in the city center of Split, just a short walk from Diocletian's Palace and other popular attractions. The museum is easily accessible on foot or by public transportation, making it an ideal stop during your exploration of Split.

Visiting the Museum: The Froggyland Museum is open daily, with varying hours depending on the season. There is a modest admission fee, which helps support the museum's upkeep and preservation. Visitors can expect to spend around an hour exploring the museum and admiring the intricately crafted dioramas.

The Froggyland Museum offers a truly unique and memorable experience for visitors of all ages. With its extensive collection of taxidermy frogs and engaging dioramas, this offbeat attraction provides a fascinating glimpse into the world of early 20th-century taxidermy and a fun, lighthearted break from Split's more traditional tourist sites.

The Jewish Cemetery

The Jewish Cemetery in Split is a historically significant site located on Marjan Hill, offering a glimpse into the city's rich cultural heritage and the Jewish community's history in the region. Established in the 16th century, the cemetery is both a serene and thought-provoking place to visit. Here are some highlights and details about the Jewish Cemetery in Split:

History: The Jewish Cemetery in Split dates back to the 16th century and was in use until the early 20th century. The site serves as a testament to the long-standing presence of the Jewish community in Split and the broader Dalmatian region. The cemetery is one of the oldest Jewish burial grounds in Europe, making it an essential site for those interested in Jewish history and heritage.

Location: Situated on Marjan Hill, the Jewish Cemetery is surrounded by lush vegetation and offers sweeping views of Split and the Adriatic Sea. The cemetery's elevated location and tranquil setting make it a peaceful retreat from the bustling city below.

Tombstones and Inscriptions: The Jewish Cemetery features a variety of tombstones, many of which display inscriptions in Hebrew, Ladino, and Italian, reflecting the diverse linguistic heritage of the Jewish community in Split. The oldest tombstones date back to the 16th century, while more recent ones date to the early 20th century. The variety of tombstone designs and inscriptions provides valuable insight into the historical and cultural context of the cemetery.

Preservation Efforts: The Jewish Cemetery in Split is protected as a cultural monument, and efforts have been made to preserve and restore the site over the years. The cemetery has faced various challenges, including natural weathering and vandalism, but ongoing restoration work has helped to maintain its historical integrity and significance.

Visiting the Cemetery: The Jewish Cemetery can be reached by walking or biking through Marjan Forest Park, following the paths that lead up the hill. The cemetery is open to the public, but visitors should be mindful of the site's cultural and religious significance and treat it with the respect it deserves.

The Jewish Cemetery in Split offers a unique and poignant look into the city's diverse cultural history and the centuries-old Jewish community in the region. A visit to the cemetery provides a peaceful and reflective experience, allowing visitors to contemplate the passage of time and the interconnectedness of different cultures in Split's rich heritage.

Kasjuni Beach

Kasjuni Beach is a beautiful and serene beach located on the western slopes of Marjan Hill in Split, Croatia. The combination of crystal-clear waters, pebbles, and sand make it a popular spot for locals and tourists alike. Here are some highlights and details about Kasjuni Beach:

Getting There: To reach Kasjuni Beach, you can walk, bike, or drive through Marjan Forest Park. The park's walking and biking trails offer a scenic route to the beach. Alternatively, you can take bus number 12 from the city center or a taxi. If you choose to drive, keep in mind that parking can be limited during peak season.

Beach Features: Kasjuni Beach has a mix of pebbles and sand, making it comfortable for sunbathing and walking. The water is crystal clear and ideal for swimming and snorkeling. The beach is surrounded by lush greenery and rocky cliffs, providing a picturesque and relaxing atmosphere.

Amenities: The beach offers various amenities, such as changing rooms, showers, and restrooms. Sun loungers and umbrellas are available for rent, ensuring a comfortable and enjoyable experience. There is also a beach bar and a restaurant serving refreshments, snacks, and local cuisine.

Water Sports and Activities: Kasjuni Beach provides opportunities for water sports and activities, such as paddleboarding, kayaking, and snorkeling. Equipment rentals are available on-site, allowing visitors to explore the nearby coves and coastlines at their leisure.

Family-Friendly: Kasjuni Beach is an excellent option for families, as it offers a calm and serene environment with shallow waters that are perfect for children to play in. The beach's relaxed atmosphere and amenities make it an ideal destination for families with young children.

Nearby Attractions:While visiting Kasjuni Beach, take the opportunity to explore the rest of Marjan Forest Park. The park features numerous walking and biking trails, historic chapels, and scenic viewpoints overlooking Split and the surrounding area. You can also visit the Mestrovic Gallery, showcasing the work of Croatian sculptor Ivan Meštrović.

Kasjuni Beach is a charming and tranquil spot that offers a perfect blend of natural beauty, recreational activities, and essential amenities. Its calm waters, stunning surroundings, and family-friendly atmosphere make it an ideal choice for those seeking a relaxing day at the beach away from Split's more crowded and touristy areas.

The Green Market (Pazar)

The Green Market, also known as "Pazar," is a vibrant and bustling outdoor market located in the heart of Split, Croatia. This lively marketplace offers a wide variety of fresh, local produce, as well as other food items, clothing, and souvenirs. Here are some highlights and details about The Green Market (Pazar) in Split:

Location: The Green Market is situated just east of the Silver Gate (Porta Argentea) of Diocletian's Palace, making it easily accessible from the city center. Its central location ensures that you can easily incorporate a visit to the market into your exploration of Split's historic sites.

Produce and Food Items: The Green Market is best known for its abundance of fresh, locally sourced fruits and vegetables. Stalls overflow with seasonal produce, including tomatoes, cucumbers, peppers, zucchini, peaches, cherries, grapes, and more. In addition to fruits and vegetables, the market also offers a variety of other food items, such as cheeses, olives, cured meats, fish, and fresh bread.

Local Experience: Visiting the Green Market is a fantastic way to immerse yourself in the local culture of Split. You'll find locals shopping for their daily groceries, as well as vendors eager to share stories and offer samples of their products. The market's lively atmosphere and friendly exchanges provide an authentic glimpse into the daily life of Split residents.

Clothing and Souvenirs: The Green Market is not limited to food items. You can also find clothing, shoes, accessories, and souvenirs at various stalls throughout the market. While some of the items may cater to tourists, you can also find unique and locally made products to take home as a reminder of your time in Split.

Opening Hours: The Green Market is open daily, usually from early morning until late afternoon. For the best selection and freshest produce, it's recommended to visit the market in the morning when the offerings are most abundant.

Tips for Visiting: When shopping at the Green Market, don't be afraid to haggle and negotiate prices, as it is a common practice at the market. Also, bring a reusable bag to carry your purchases and a handful of small bills or coins to make transactions easier.

The Green Market (Pazar) in Split offers a vibrant and authentic experience for visitors, allowing you to discover and taste the freshest local produce while engaging with the local community. Whether you're in search of delicious ingredients for a picnic or unique souvenirs to take home, the Green Market provides a lively and memorable experience in the heart of Split.

By exploring these hidden gems in Split, you'll be able to experience the city from a unique perspective and create lasting memories of your time in this captivating destination. The off-the-beaten-path attractions and experiences described in Chapter 6 provide an alternative way to discover the city, ensuring that your visit to Split is truly unforgettable.

Split Travel Guide 2023 And Beyond

Lesser Known Attraction

Borislav Blagoje

CHAPTER SEVEN

Best Day Trips from Split

Split, Croatia is located in a prime location for exploring some of the beautiful islands and towns that are located nearby. Here are some of the best day trips from Split:

Hvar Island

Hvar Island is one of the most popular day trips from Split, located off the coast of Croatia in the Adriatic Sea. The island is known for its stunning natural beauty, crystal-clear waters, and vibrant nightlife. Here are some more details about Hvar Island:

Hvar Island is known for its beautiful beaches, including the famous Zlatni Rat Beach, which is a narrow, pebble beach that stretches out into the sea. Other popular beaches on the island include Dubovica Beach, Milna Beach, and Pokonji Dol Beach, all of which offer crystal-clear waters and stunning scenery.

Hvar Island is home to several charming towns and villages, including Hvar Town, Stari Grad, Jelsa, and Vrboska. These towns are known for their historic architecture, charming streets, and local specialties, such as lavender products and olive oil.

Hvar Island is also known for its vibrant nightlife, with a wide range of bars, clubs, and restaurants offering entertainment late into the night. Hvar Town is particularly known for its lively nightlife, with clubs such as Carpe Diem and Hula Hula Beach Club drawing visitors from all over the world.

Hvar Island has a rich history and culture, with several historic sites and monuments to explore. The island's historic sites include the Hvar Fortress, Stari Grad Plain (a UNESCO World Heritage Site), and the Franciscan Monastery in Hvar Town.

Split Travel Guide 2023 And Beyond

Hvar Island offers a wide range of outdoor activities, including hiking, cycling, kayaking, and sailing. Visitors can explore the island's beautiful natural landscapes, including its forests, vineyards, and olive groves.

Hvar Island is a must-visit destination for anyone traveling to Croatia, with its stunning natural beauty, vibrant nightlife, and rich history and culture. Whether you are interested in relaxing on the beach, exploring historic sites, or enjoying outdoor activities, Hvar Island has something to offer for everyone.

Brac Island

Brac Island is a popular day trip destination from Split, located in the Adriatic Sea off the coast of Croatia. The island is known for its stunning beaches, crystal-clear waters, and charming towns and villages. Here are some more details about Brac Island:

Brac Island is famous for its beautiful beaches, including the famous Zlatni Rat Beach, which is a narrow, pebble beach that changes shape with the wind and currents. Other popular beaches on the island include Supetar Beach, Povlja Beach, and Lovrecina Bay, all of which offer crystal-clear waters and stunning scenery.

Brac Island is home to several charming towns and villages, including Supetar, Bol, Milna, and Pucisca. These towns are known for their historic architecture, narrow streets, and local specialties, such as olive oil, wine, and figs.

Brac Island offers a wide range of outdoor activities, including hiking, cycling, and water sports such as windsurfing and kiteboarding. Visitors can explore the island's beautiful natural landscapes, including its forests, vineyards, and olive groves.

Brac Island has a rich history, and visitors can explore several historic sites and monuments on the island. These sites include the Vidova Gora Mountain, the Dominican Monastery in Bol, and the Blaca Hermitage, which is a 16th-century monastery carved into a cliffside.

Brac Island is known for its delicious local cuisine, which includes fresh seafood, lamb, and locally produced olive oil and wine. Visitors can try traditional dishes such as pašticada (a slow-cooked beef stew) and brudet (a seafood stew), as well as local specialties such as the Brača Varenik, a type of sweet vinegar made from wine.

Brac Island is a beautiful and diverse destination, with something to offer for everyone. Whether you are interested in relaxing on the beach, exploring historic sites, or enjoying outdoor activities, Brac Island is definitely worth a visit.

Trogir

Trogir is a historic town located just a short drive from Split, making it an ideal day trip destination. The town is known for its charming old town, historic sites, and beautiful architecture. Here are some more details about Trogir:

Trogir's old town is a UNESCO World Heritage Site and is known for its narrow streets, historic buildings, and charming squares. Visitors can explore the town's historic landmarks, such as the St. Lawrence Cathedral, the Kamerlengo Fortress, and the Duke's Palace.

Trogir was once ruled by the Venetians, and the town's architecture and culture still reflect this influence. The town's historic landmarks feature a unique blend of Venetian, Romanesque, and Renaissance styles.

Trogir's marina is a popular spot for yachting and sailing, and visitors can enjoy the stunning views of the town's historic buildings and the nearby islands.

Trogir is known for its delicious cuisine, which includes fresh seafood, traditional Dalmatian dishes, and locally produced wine. Visitors can try local specialties such as pašticada (a slow-cooked beef stew), octopus salad, and peka (a meat and vegetable dish cooked under a bell-shaped lid).

Trogir is located close to several beautiful islands, including Drvenik Veli, Drvenik Mali, and Solta Island. Visitors can take a boat tour to explore these islands' stunning beaches, crystal-clear waters, and picturesque villages.

Trogir is a charming and historic town that offers visitors a glimpse into Croatia's rich history and culture. Whether you are interested in history, culture, or outdoor activities, Trogir is definitely worth a visit.

Omis

Omis is a small town located at the mouth of the Cetina River, just a short drive from Split. The town is known for its stunning natural beauty, including its sandy beaches, crystal-clear waters, and dramatic cliffs. Here are some more details about Omis:

Omis is known for its beautiful beaches, including the Omis City Beach, which is a long, sandy beach with crystal-clear waters. Other popular beaches in Omis include Nemira Beach, Brzet Beach, and Velika Luka Beach.

Omis offers a wide range of outdoor activities, including hiking, cycling, kayaking, and rock climbing. Visitors can explore the town's beautiful natural landscapes, including its forests, canyons, and mountains.

The Cetina River is a popular spot for rafting and kayaking, with stunning views of the surrounding mountains and canyons. Visitors can take a boat tour or rent a kayak to explore the river's natural beauty.

Omis has a rich history, and visitors can explore several historic sites and monuments in the town, including the Starigrad Fortress and the Mirabella Fortress. These fortresses offer stunning views of the town and the Adriatic Sea.

Omis is known for its delicious local cuisine, which includes fresh seafood, lamb, and locally produced olive oil and wine. Visitors can try traditional dishes such as pasticada (a slow-cooked beef stew) and brudet (a seafood stew), as well as local specialties such as Omis prosciutto and Omis cherry liqueur.

Omis is a beautiful and diverse destination, with something to offer for everyone. Whether you are interested in relaxing on the beach, exploring historic sites, or enjoying outdoor activities, Omis is definitely worth a visit.

Krka National Park

Krka National Park is a stunning natural park located about an hour's drive from Split. The park is known for its beautiful waterfalls, pristine lakes, and lush forests, and visitors can enjoy hiking, swimming, and boat tours to explore its natural beauty. Here are some more details about Krka National Park:

Krka National Park is home to several stunning waterfalls, including Skradinski Buk, which is one of the park's most famous and largest waterfalls. Visitors can also explore other waterfalls, such as Roski Slap and Manojlovacki Slap, which offer beautiful views of the park's natural landscapes.

Krka National Park is home to several beautiful lakes, including Visovac Lake, which is located on a small island in the middle of the park. Visitors can take a boat tour to explore the lake's stunning scenery and learn about the island's history.

Krka National Park offers several hiking trails that allow visitors to explore the park's natural beauty on foot. These trails range from easy to challenging, and offer stunning views of the park's waterfalls, lakes, and forests.

Visitors can swim in several locations within the park, including at Skradinski Buk waterfall and Roski Slap waterfall. The park's crystal-clear waters are ideal for swimming, and visitors can also enjoy snorkeling and diving.

Krka National Park is home to several historic sites, including the Krka Monastery, which is located near Skradinski Buk waterfall. Visitors can also explore the park's ethnographic collection, which showcases the traditional way of life in the region.

Krka National Park is a stunning natural park that offers visitors a chance to explore some of Croatia's most beautiful natural landscapes. Whether you are interested in hiking, swimming, or simply enjoying the park's natural beauty, Krka National Park is definitely worth a visit.

Dubrovnik

Dubrovnik is a historic coastal city located in southern Croatia, known for its stunning Old Town, medieval walls, and beautiful beaches. Here are some more details about Dubrovnik:

Dubrovnik's Old Town is a UNESCO World Heritage Site and is known for its well-preserved medieval walls, narrow streets, and historic buildings. Visitors can explore the town's historic landmarks, such as the Dubrovnik Cathedral, the Rector's Palace, and the Sponza Palace.

Split Travel Guide 2023 And Beyond

Dubrovnik's city walls are one of the town's most iconic landmarks, and offer stunning views of the town and the Adriatic Sea. Visitors can take a walk along the walls and explore the towers and fortresses that were used to defend the town.

Dubrovnik is home to several beautiful beaches, including Banje Beach, which is located just outside the Old Town and offers stunning views of the town's medieval walls. Other popular beaches in Dubrovnik include Lapad Beach, Copacabana Beach, and Sveti Jakov Beach.

The Dubrovnik Cable Car is a popular attraction that offers stunning views of the town and the Adriatic Sea. Visitors can take a cable car ride up to the top of Mount Srd and enjoy panoramic views of Dubrovnik and the surrounding area.

Dubrovnik is located close to several beautiful islands, including the Elaphiti Islands and the island of Mljet. Visitors can take a boat tour to explore these islands' stunning beaches, crystal-clear waters, and picturesque villages.

Dubrovnik is known for its delicious local cuisine, which includes fresh seafood, traditional Dalmatian dishes, and locally produced wine. Visitors can try local specialties such as black risotto, octopus salad, and pasticada (a slow-cooked beef stew).

Dubrovnik is a beautiful and historic city that offers visitors a glimpse into Croatia's rich history and culture. Whether you are interested in history, culture, or outdoor activities, Dubrovnik is definitely worth a visit.

There are many great day trips from Split that offer visitors a chance to explore the beautiful islands, towns, and natural landscapes of Croatia. Whether you are interested in history, culture, or outdoor activities, there is something for everyone to enjoy on a day trip from Split.

Split Travel Guide 2023 And Beyond

Map Of Day Trip From Split

Borislav Blagoje

CHAPTER EIGHT

Practical Information

In this chapter, we provide essential practical information to help you navigate Split, Croatia with ease and make the most of your visit. From understanding local customs to knowing where to find vital services, this chapter covers the necessary details for a smooth and enjoyable stay in Split.

Currency and Money Exchange

When visiting Split, Croatia, it's essential to understand the local currency, where to exchange money, and how to manage your finances during your trip. Here's a closer look at currency and money exchange in Split:

Local Currency: The official currency in Croatia is the Croatian Kuna (HRK). The Kuna is subdivided into 100 Lipa. Banknotes come in denominations of 10, 20, 50, 100, 200, 500, and 1,000 Kuna.

Money Exchange Options:

Banks: Most banks in Split offer currency exchange services. They usually offer competitive exchange rates and charge a small commission. Banks are typically open from Monday to Friday, with some also open on Saturday mornings.

Exchange Offices: You'll find numerous exchange offices (Mjenjačnica) throughout Split, especially in the city center and tourist areas. While they often provide convenient services, their exchange rates and fees may vary, so it's a good idea to compare rates before exchanging money.

ATMs: Many visitors find using ATMs to be the most convenient way to obtain local currency. ATMs are widely available throughout Split and often offer competitive exchange rates. Keep in mind that your home bank and the Croatian bank may charge fees for withdrawals or currency conversion. It's a good idea to check with your bank regarding any fees before your trip.

Credit and Debit Cards:

Most hotels, restaurants, and shops in Split accept major credit and debit cards, such as Visa, Mastercard, and, to a lesser extent, American Express. However, smaller establishments and outdoor markets may only accept cash. It's always a good idea to carry some cash with you for smaller purchases and emergencies.

Traveler's Checks: Traveler's checks are becoming less common and may not be accepted at many establishments in Split. It's recommended to rely on cash, credit cards, and debit cards instead.

Tips for Managing Money in Split

Check exchange rates and fees before exchanging money to ensure you're getting the best deal possible.

Keep a mix of cash and cards on hand to be prepared for various situations.

Inform your bank and credit card company of your travel plans to avoid any issues with card usage or fraud alerts.

Always carry a small amount of local currency in small denominations for minor purchases, tipping, or emergencies.

Understanding the local currency and money exchange options in Split will help you manage your finances during your trip and avoid any unexpected surprises. By being well-prepared, you can focus on enjoying your time in this beautiful Croatian city.

Transportation

Split is a walkable city, with many of its main attractions located within a comfortable walking distance from one another. However, there are various modes of transportation available in Split to help you navigate the city and its surroundings. Here's a closer look at transportation options in Split:

Walking: Exploring Split on foot is an excellent way to immerse yourself in the city's atmosphere and discover hidden gems. The city center, including Diocletian's Palace, the Riva Promenade, and Marjan Hill, is easily accessible by foot. Pedestrian-friendly streets and the compact nature of the city center make walking a popular choice for visitors.

Public Buses: The public bus system in Split is operated by Promet Split and offers an extensive network of routes throughout the city and its surrounding areas. Bus tickets can be purchased at kiosks, on board the bus (at a slightly higher price), or via the Promet Split mobile app. Single-ride tickets and daily or multi-day passes are available.

Taxis and Rideshare Services: Taxis are readily available in Split and can be hailed on the street, found at taxi stands, or booked in advance. Reputable taxi companies include Radio Taxi Split and

Taxi Cammeo. Rideshare services, such as Uber, are also available in Split, offering a convenient alternative to traditional taxis.

Bicycles: Biking is a popular and eco-friendly way to explore Split and its surroundings. Numerous bike rental shops offer a range of bicycles, including city bikes, mountain bikes, and electric bikes. Marjan Hill and the surrounding coastline offer scenic bike routes for visitors to enjoy.

Car Rentals: Renting a car in Split is a convenient option for those who plan to explore the surrounding areas or embark on road trips. Several car rental agencies, including international brands and local companies, operate in Split. Keep in mind that parking in the city center can be challenging and expensive, so a car may not be necessary if you're primarily exploring the city on foot.

Ferries and Catamarans: Split is a gateway to the beautiful Croatian islands, such as Hvar, Brač, and Vis. Regular ferries and catamarans, operated by companies like Jadrolinija and Krilo, connect Split with various islands and coastal towns. Tickets can be purchased online, at the ferry terminal, or through local travel agencies.

Airport Transfers: Split Airport (SPU) is located approximately 24 km (15 miles) from the city center. Various transportation options are available for getting to and from the airport, including airport shuttle buses, public buses, taxis, and private transfers.

Understanding the transportation options in Split will help you make informed decisions about how to navigate the city and its surroundings. By choosing the most suitable mode of transport, you can make the most of your time in Split and explore all that this beautiful Croatian city has to offer.

Language

The official language of Croatia is Croatian, which is part of the Slavic language family and uses the Latin alphabet. In Split, you will find that many locals, especially those working in the tourism industry, speak English quite well. However, it is always appreciated when visitors make an effort to learn some basic phrases in the local language. Here's a closer look at the language situation in Split:

English Proficiency: Croatia ranks high in terms of English proficiency among non-native English-speaking countries. In Split, a popular tourist destination, you can expect a significant number of locals to speak English, particularly in hotels, restaurants, and tourist attractions. Younger generations tend to have a better command of English due to its prevalence in education and exposure to English-speaking media.

Other Languages: Besides English, some Croatians also speak other languages, such as German, Italian, or French, as second or third languages. This is especially true for those working in the tourism sector or those who have studied or worked abroad. Additionally, due to the proximity and shared history with neighboring countries, some Croatians may speak languages such as Serbian or Bosnian.

Basic Croatian Phrases: While many locals in Split speak English, it's always a good idea to learn a few basic Croatian phrases to help you navigate the city and interact with locals. Here are some useful phrases:

Hello: Bok or Dobar dan

Goodbye: Doviđenja

Please: Molim

Thank you: Hvala

Excuse me: Oprostite

Yes: Da

No: Ne

Do you speak English?: Govorite li engleski?

Language Tips:

Carry a small Croatian phrasebook or download a language app on your phone to help with translations and communication.

Don't be afraid to ask locals for help with pronunciation or translations. Most Croatians are friendly and more than happy to assist you.

When speaking to locals in English, try to speak slowly and clearly to ensure they understand you.

Understanding the language situation in Split, Croatia, will help you communicate more effectively during your visit. By learning some basic Croatian phrases and being open to engaging with locals, you can enhance your travel experience and create lasting memories in this beautiful city.

Weather and Climate

Split enjoys a Mediterranean climate, characterized by hot, dry summers and mild, wet winters. The city benefits from plenty of sunshine throughout the year, making it an attractive destination for tourists. Here's a closer look at the weather and climate in Split:

Summer (June to August): Summers in Split are typically hot and dry, with average high temperatures ranging from 27°C (81°F) to 30°C (86°F). The peak summer months of July and August are the hottest, and also the busiest months for tourism. During this time, you can expect long days with up to 12-14 hours of sunlight, perfect for beachgoers and sunseekers. Rainfall is minimal, averaging around 20-30mm per month.

Autumn (September to November): Autumn in Split is generally mild and pleasant, with temperatures gradually cooling down from the hot summer months. September still offers warm weather, with average high temperatures around 24°C (75°F), making it an ideal time for outdoor activities and exploring the city without the summer crowds. As the season progresses, temperatures continue to decrease, and rainfall becomes more frequent, especially in November.

Winter (December to February): Winters in Split are mild compared to other parts of Europe, with average high temperatures ranging from 10°C (50°F) to 13°C (55°F). Low temperatures can drop to around 5°C (41°F) during the coldest months of January and February. Winter is the wettest season, with rainfall averaging between 80-110mm per month. Snow is rare in Split, but it can occasionally occur in the surrounding mountains.

Spring (March to May): Spring is a beautiful time to visit Split, as temperatures gradually warm up and the city comes alive with blooming flowers and lush greenery. Average high temperatures range from 15°C (59°F) in March to 21°C (70°F) in May. Rainfall decreases throughout the spring months, making way for sunnier days and more predictable weather.

Best Time to Visit:

The best time to visit Split depends on your preferences and the activities you plan to do. For beach lovers and sunseekers, the summer months offer the warmest weather and plenty of sunshine. However, it's also the busiest time for tourism, so expect higher prices and more crowded attractions.

For those who prefer milder temperatures and fewer crowds, the shoulder seasons of spring (April-May) and autumn (September-October) are ideal. During these months, the weather is generally pleasant, and you can explore the city and its surroundings more comfortably.

If you don't mind cooler temperatures and more rainfall, the winter months can offer a different perspective on Split, with fewer tourists and lower prices for accommodations and attractions.

Understanding the weather and climate in Split, Croatia, will help you plan your trip accordingly and ensure you're prepared for the local conditions. By choosing the right time to visit based on your preferences, you can make the most of your time in this stunning coastal city.

Safety and Emergency Services

Split is generally considered a safe destination for tourists, with low crime rates and a welcoming atmosphere. However, as with any destination, it's essential to remain vigilant and take necessary precautions to ensure a safe and enjoyable visit. Here's a closer look at safety and emergency services in Split:

General Safety Tips:

Keep your belongings secure and be aware of your surroundings, especially in crowded areas or tourist hotspots, where pickpocketing can occur.

Use caution when withdrawing money from ATMs, and try to use machines located in well-lit areas or inside banks.

Avoid walking alone in poorly lit or unfamiliar areas, particularly at night.

When using taxis, choose reputable companies or use rideshare apps like Uber to ensure a safe and reliable ride.

Be cautious when swimming in the sea, as there can be strong currents. Always follow local beach safety guidelines and swim in designated areas.

Emergency Numbers:

In the event of an emergency, it's important to know the local emergency numbers. Here are the essential numbers to remember:

General emergency number: 112 (This number can be used for any emergency, including police, medical, and fire emergencies)

Police: 192

Ambulance: 194

Fire department: 193

These numbers can be dialed from any phone, including mobile phones, and are toll-free.

Medical Services:

In case of a medical emergency, Split has a number of hospitals and medical centers equipped to handle various situations. The main hospital in Split is the University Hospital Center Split (KBC Split), located at Spinčićeva 1. There are also numerous pharmacies (called "ljekarna" in Croatian) throughout the city, where you can purchase over-the-counter medications and seek advice from pharmacists.

Police: The main police station in Split is located at Ul. kralja Zvonimira 39. In case of an emergency or if you need assistance, you can contact the police at the emergency number 192.

Consulates and Embassies: If you require assistance from your country's diplomatic representation while in Split, you may need to visit the nearest embassy or consulate in Zagreb, the capital of Croatia. Some countries have honorary consulates in Split, which can offer limited assistance in certain situations.

By being aware of safety precautions and knowing how to access emergency services in Split, Croatia, you can have a safe and enjoyable trip. Always remain vigilant and follow local advice to ensure a pleasant experience in this beautiful coastal city.

Healthcare and Pharmacies

Croatia has a well-developed healthcare system, with public and private medical facilities available throughout the country. Split, as a major city, offers a range of healthcare services for locals and visitors alike. Here's a closer look at healthcare and pharmacies in Split:

Healthcare Facilities:

In case of a medical emergency or if you require medical assistance during your visit to Split, the city has several healthcare facilities to cater to your needs. The main hospital in Split is the University Hospital Center Split (KBC Split), located at Spinčićeva 1. This hospital is equipped to handle various medical situations and emergencies.

In addition to the main hospital, there are several smaller clinics and private medical practices throughout the city that offer a range of services, including general practitioners, dentists, and specialists.

Pharmacies:

Pharmacies in Croatia are called "ljekarna" and are easily identifiable by their green cross signage. Split has numerous pharmacies throughout the city, including some that operate 24 hours a day. Pharmacies generally carry a wide range of over-the-counter medications, prescription drugs, and other healthcare items.

Some pharmacies in Split offer a 24-hour service on a rotating basis. To find the nearest 24-hour pharmacy, you can check local listings, ask at your accommodation, or inquire at any pharmacy, as they usually display a list of the closest 24-hour pharmacy locations.

Croatian pharmacists are well-trained and can provide advice on minor ailments and recommend over-the-counter medications when appropriate. For prescription medications, you will need a prescription from a local doctor.

Health Insurance and Payment:

Before traveling to Croatia, it is essential to ensure you have appropriate travel health insurance to cover any potential medical expenses during your trip. While Croatia has reciprocal healthcare agreements with some countries, these agreements may not cover all medical costs or services, and private travel insurance is still recommended.

If you are an EU citizen, you should obtain a European Health Insurance Card (EHIC) before traveling, which will grant you access to state-provided healthcare during your stay in Croatia. However, the EHIC may not cover all medical expenses, so additional travel insurance is advised.

Private healthcare providers in Split may require upfront payment or a guarantee of payment from your insurance company before providing treatment. Make sure you understand your insurance coverage and keep all receipts and documents for reimbursement purposes.

Being prepared and knowledgeable about healthcare services and pharmacies in Split, Croatia, will ensure that you have access to medical assistance if needed during your trip. Always carry your travel insurance and relevant medical documents with you, and familiarize yourself with the locations of nearby medical facilities and pharmacies to have a safe and enjoyable visit to this beautiful city.

Electrical Outlets

When traveling to a foreign country, it's essential to be aware of the type of electrical outlets used and the local voltage to ensure your electronic devices are compatible. In Split, Croatia, the electrical outlets and voltage are the same as the rest of the country. Here's a closer look at the electrical outlets in Split:

Voltage: The standard voltage in Croatia is 230 volts, with a frequency of 50 Hz. This voltage is similar to the rest of Europe and compatible with many electronic devices. However, if you're coming from a country that uses a different voltage, such as the United States (120 volts) or Japan (100 volts), you may need a voltage converter or transformer to use your devices safely.

Electrical Outlets:

In Split, as well as the rest of Croatia, the electrical outlets are of Type F, also known as "Schuko" plugs. These outlets have two round pins and are compatible with both Type C (European 2-pin) and Type E (French) plugs.

If your electronic devices have plugs that do not match Type F outlets, you will need a travel adapter to use them in Croatia. It's recommended to purchase a universal travel adapter before your trip, as these adapters can be harder to find or more expensive in tourist areas.

Power Surges and Fluctuations: While power surges and fluctuations are not common in Croatia, they can still occur. If you're traveling with sensitive electronic devices, such as laptops or cameras, it's a good idea to use a surge protector to prevent potential damage.

Charging Electronic Devices: Keep in mind that charging times for your devices may vary depending on the voltage in Croatia. If your device is designed for a lower voltage, it may take longer to charge, while devices designed for higher voltages may charge more quickly.

By understanding the electrical outlets and voltage in Split, Croatia, you can ensure your electronic devices are compatible and avoid any potential issues during your trip. Remember to pack a travel adapter or voltage converter if necessary, and consider using a surge protector for sensitive devices to keep them safe and functioning properly.

Wi-Fi and Internet Access

In today's digitally connected world, having access to the internet while traveling is essential for many tourists. Split, Croatia, offers various options for Wi-Fi and internet access to keep you connected during your trip. Here's a closer look at Wi-Fi and internet access in Split:

Free Wi-Fi Hotspots: Split offers numerous free Wi-Fi hotspots throughout the city, particularly in popular tourist areas and public spaces. The city center, including the Riva promenade and Diocletian's Palace, has free Wi-Fi coverage for visitors. To connect, simply look for the "Split Wi-Fi" network and follow the on-screen instructions to register.

Cafes, Restaurants, and Bars: Many cafes, restaurants, and bars in Split offer free Wi-Fi to their customers. Simply ask the staff for the Wi-Fi password or check your receipt, as it is sometimes printed there. Keep in mind that the connection speeds may vary depending on the location and the number of users connected.

Hotels and Accommodations: Most hotels, hostels, and vacation rentals in Split provide free Wi-Fi to their guests. The connection speed and quality may vary depending on the type of accommodation and the number of guests using the network. Some establishments may also offer wired internet connections in guest rooms for a more stable connection.

Public Libraries and Cultural Centers: Public libraries and cultural centers in Split often have free Wi-Fi available for visitors. These locations can provide a quiet and comfortable environment to work or browse the internet. Be sure to check the opening hours and any specific rules for using the facilities.

Mobile Data and SIM Cards: If you require more reliable internet access or plan to use data-intensive applications during your trip, consider purchasing a local SIM card with a data plan. Croatian mobile networks, such as T-Mobile, A1, and Tele2, offer prepaid SIM cards with various data options. You can find SIM cards at mobile network stores, supermarkets, and kiosks throughout the city. Make sure your phone is unlocked and compatible with the local network frequencies before purchasing a SIM card.

By understanding the various options for Wi-Fi and internet access in Split, Croatia, you can stay connected throughout your trip. From free public Wi-Fi to local SIM cards, there are plenty of ways to keep in touch with friends, family, and work while enjoying your time in this beautiful coastal city.

This chapter aims to provide you with essential practical information to help you navigate Split, Croatia comfortably and efficiently. By being well-prepared and informed, you can focus on

Split Travel Guide 2023 And Beyond

enjoying the incredible experiences and attractions that Split has to offer.

CHAPTER NINE

Conclusion

Final Thoughts and Farewells

As we conclude our journey through Split Travel Guide 2023: A Handbook for Exploring the Best of Split, Croatia and its Surroundings, we hope that this guide has provided you with valuable insights and tips to make the most of your visit to this enchanting coastal city.

From its rich history and stunning architecture to the vibrant culinary scene, Split offers a wealth of experiences that will captivate your senses and leave a lasting impression. The city's unique blend of ancient and modern, combined with its inviting atmosphere, ensures that there's always something to discover and enjoy.

Beyond the city limits, the surrounding region offers even more opportunities for exploration, with idyllic islands, pristine beaches, and picturesque towns just a short journey away. Each destination has its own charm and allure, inviting you to uncover the hidden gems of the Dalmatian Coast.

As you prepare for your trip, remember to revisit the practical information and tips provided throughout this guide, from transportation and accommodations to safety and cultural etiquette. Being well-informed and prepared will ensure a smoother and more enjoyable journey, allowing you to focus on the experiences that await you in Split and beyond.

Lastly, we encourage you to embrace the spirit of adventure and curiosity during your visit. Split and its surroundings are a treasure trove of stories, traditions, and natural beauty, just waiting to be uncovered. Whether you're wandering the ancient streets of Diocletian's Palace, hiking the verdant trails of Marjan Hill, or sipping on local wine while watching the sun set over the Adriatic Sea, every moment in Split is an opportunity to create unforgettable memories.

As you embark on your adventure, we wish you a wonderful and fulfilling journey, and we hope that Split Travel Guide 2023 has been a valuable companion in planning your trip. Safe travels, and may the beauty of Split, Croatia and its surroundings captivate your heart and soul for years to come.

Borislav Blagoje

Printed in Great Britain
by Amazon